# INTERNSHIP
# MASTERY

# INTERNSHIP MASTERY

The Technology Student's Guide to
Crushing Your Internship and
Launching Your Career

RYAN D. GLICK

This book is dedicated to my mom and dad, who showed me that hard work and commitment to helping others always comes full circle. And to my wife, Kristin, and our children, Jacob, William, and Hannah, for putting up with my crazy office hours and time commitment it took to write this book. Without you, this book wouldn't have been possible.

# Table of Contents

# Preface

The year was 2000, and I was heading off to the University of Iowa to start my college career. I hadn't given any thought to what I was going to do after school. I mean, why would I? College was supposed to be all about the experience, after all—or so I thought. As time went on, though, I slowly built an understanding of what I wanted to do when I graduated. I really enjoyed my business courses, and technology (specifically software development) was fascinating to me. Yet the last thing on my mind at any point throughout college was looking for a summer internship.

So four years later, in 2004, I walked across the stage in a crowded auditorium to receive my diploma: a Bachelor of Business Administration (BBA) in management information systems. I also managed to earn a minor in computer science (and later, in 2009, a Master of Business Administration, or MBA). With my BBA in hand and no summer internship experience, I headed out into the "real" world to start my life.

From 2004 to 2006, I worked for my oldest brother at his web design, web hosting, and information technology company. With no prior business or industry experience to hang my hat on, I made a lot of naive assumptions and mistakes.

Since 2006, I have spent many years in the Fortune 500 business world—first as a software engineer, and then as an information technology leader. Over the years, I've interviewed hundreds of intern candidates and hired a select few of them, and I'm always intrigued by the process. Why are some candidates so well prepared, while others seem to be simply going through the motions? Why do some interns take full advantage of their internship experiences, while others seem to blend in with the crowd and then disappear when their time at the company comes to an end?

The more I reflected on this phenomenon, the more I wanted to help college students make the most out of their internships. The truth is, an internship can be a gold mine of experience and connections, and it can springboard you into a successful future. However, this is only possible if you are adequately prepared. It's not rocket science, as you'll see in the coming pages, but it does take some brainpower and ambition.

This is exactly the reason I wrote this book. Not only do I want you to land a great technology internship, I want your entire internship experience to be a positive one. I want your internship to be more than a one-liner on your resume. I want you to kick-start your journey toward the career of your dreams. Whether you plan to be a tech entrepreneur and start your own business or work your way up within a large organization, my plan can help you.

You can access all of the free Internship Mastery Insider Resources that are mentioned throughout this book at the following link: https://ryanglick.com/intern-resources. You'll also find other resources I have for students like you to successfully land and navigate their internships.

I want to personally thank you for letting me join you on your internship journey. It means a lot to me that you are here.

# Introduction

As the door slowly opened, the cool, dry air hit me square in the face. I walked nervously into a large, highly secured room where hundreds of servers and other pieces of equipment were humming like a swarm of locusts. I walked as confidently as possible toward a piece of multimillion-dollar equipment that I was there to perform "surgery" on. I carried a large cardboard box containing several expensive parts, and I had a bag slung over my shoulder with a single—yet very important—instruction manual. A sense of relief came over me for a moment as the guy who guided me to the equipment left me by myself to do my work. The last thing I wanted to do was stumble my way through the job while someone watched me. Then the nervousness resumed when I realized I was still being watched. There were at least a dozen cameras pointed at me from every direction. Well, maybe not truly pointed at me specifically, but it felt that way.

"What am I doing here?" I asked myself.

You may be asking this same question as you prepare for your first internship. It may be scary. You may be intimidated. You may be nervous. Those feelings are all perfectly normal. Rest assured, your confidence will grow and your nerves will subside as you develop your internship plan in the coming pages.

So what is an internship anyway? That's easy: it's the perfect resume-builder that will help you land your dream job after you graduate from college. Okay, we both know that isn't true. Unfortunately, this is the mindset of many college students who are out looking for anything and everything to boost their resumes. The problem? Businesses are caring less and less about what your resume says these days. Businesses want to know what you've *actually* done—and if you've had an internship, what you did during your time there. Not what your team did. What *you* did. How did you take advantage of the opportunity? What value did you provide to the organization? What innovative projects or solutions did you work on or suggest? How did you go above and beyond your position's expectations?

I've interviewed countless technology intern candidates over the years, and it's amazing how many appear lost and unprepared. They continually stumble for the right responses to trivial questions. They don't even know why they want internships. They often flat-out admit that a buddy of theirs (or a parent) told them it would be a good idea to get an internship. And that's it. They are there because someone told them to do it. Not because they see the potential value it can create in their own lives and careers or the value they can bring to the company.

Then there is the tiny fraction of candidates who seem like they have it all figured out. They've planned out the purpose of their internships. They know what they'd like to get out of them. They even know all the right things to say, and they speak with confidence throughout their interviews. Even so, not all interns who nail their interviews excel when they step into the corporate or business environment. Over the years, some of my interns excelled and were even brought on as full-time team members, while others failed to take advantage of their internship opportunities.

Why the difference? The chapters that follow will help you understand. Regardless of whether you've already landed an internship or you've yet to start searching for one, this book will help you acquire all the tools necessary to go into your internship with confidence and rock it. And it won't end there. When you leave your internship, you'll know exactly what to do with the experience and knowledge you've gained.

Back to my story from the beginning of this section. A week prior, I had received a phone call from an out-of-state technology company asking for my small business's help fixing some equipment at a large insurance company that they contracted with in my area. I had zero experience working on this equipment. So I did what any ambitious twenty-five-year-old information technology (IT) person would do. I said, "Sure! Just let me know when and where."

It wasn't easy, and I needed plenty of help from the instruction manual and vendor phone support, but I ended up successfully fixing the equipment. The technology company that had hired me called many more times over the years because of that first successful job. All it took was for me to take a chance and say yes.

Are you ready to take a chance and dive into this book with me? Cool. Let's get started!

## HOW THIS BOOK IS STRUCTURED

To make it as easy as possible to navigate this book, I've organized it into four clearly defined parts:

- **Part 1: Before Your Internship.** What do you need to do before your internship begins?
- **Part 2: During Your Internship.** What steps should you take during your internship to make the most out of the experience?
- **Part 3: After Your Internship.** What action should you take once your internship comes to an end to ensure you ride your wave of momentum?
- **Part 4: Accelerate Your Growth.** How can you leverage personal and professional growth to find your fast lane toward life and career success?

At the end of each chapter, you will find a section labeled **Take Action**, offering a summarized list of the most important action items for that chapter.

# PART 1:

# Before Your Internship

In this first part of the book, we're going to cover all the considerations and action items you need to be aware of before you start an internship. Regardless of whether you have an internship lined up or not, this part of the book has valuable insights that will help you:

- Define your internship goals and objectives
- Prepare your resume and cover letter
- Find the right internship for you
- Apply for your ideal internship
- Nail your interview

# CHAPTER 1

# Define Your Goals
# and Objectives

*There is one quality which one must possess to win, and that is
definiteness of purpose, the knowledge of what one wants, and
a burning desire to possess it.* —Napoleon Hill, author

L et's face it: planning can be super boring. It's much more fun
to get after it and get things done. Why take the time to put
together a plan—especially for something as seemingly trivial as
an internship?

Here are the facts. We're not all the same. We don't have
the same future goals. We don't have the same level of ambition
and determination. Not only are *we* all different; internships are
different, too. This is why outlining your goals and objectives is
important to your success.

Before we get into the details, head over to the Internship
Mastery Insider Resources page, where you can access the workbook that you'll fill out as you go through this book. You can find
both digital and printable versions here: https://ryanglick.com/
intern-resources.

## YOUR FUTURE CAREER

Think about the next five years. Will you be working for a company for the next five years? Or will you branch out on your own at some point? This is the most important question in choosing the right internship. If you're an entrepreneurial person and you plan to branch out and start your own business within the next five years, then this is important to note. If you're after the security of a stable career with a larger organization, then this is also important to note. Ultimately, you're going to use this information to ensure you find the right internship, which we'll discuss in more detail when we get to Chapter 3. Okay, fill out the first part of the workbook with your five-year career objective.

## PERSONALITY TEST

A great tool for self-analysis as we go through the next couple of sections is to spend five to ten minutes taking the free Myers Briggs online personality test you can access from here: https://ryanglick.com/personality-test. I know this doesn't sound like a lot of fun, yet you'll find that this test is surprisingly accurate and helpful. You can even take it multiple times to confirm your results are consistent.

Now that you've taken your personality test, what did you think? Did your assigned personality type describe you accurately? I've taken this personality test on multiple occasions, and it's almost creepy how closely it describes my strengths, weaknesses, and other traits. In case you're interested, I'm a "Turbulent Architect"—INTJ-T. Are you similar?

Take a look at your results in detail. Check out the various sections for your personality type. By analyzing your results, you'll not only learn about your self, but also about personality types and how best to work with them. This will be helpful during your internship and as you start your career. I'd encourage you to take this personality test again when you finish your internship to see if your personality has changed at all.

## STRENGTHS AND WEAKNESSES

I'm sure you've heard enough about strengths and weaknesses to make your head spin. I know I have. I definitely remember non-stop talk about it when I was in college. As much as you might think it's all just fluff (and some of it can be), there's real value in exploring your strengths and weaknesses when you do it right. Let me explain with a story about a fictional intern. We'll call him Ted.

Ted is a third-year student at a local state college. He's somewhat introverted and hardworking, and he's following in his dad's footsteps to become a software engineer. Ted is the stereotypical software engineer—quiet, reserved, and keeps to himself. He has no interest in speaking in front of large groups. He wants to spend his time in small groups or alone, writing lines of code. Today's conventional wisdom tells Ted that he should ignore his primary weakness (shyness) and double down on his primary strengths (hardworking and innovative). So Ted continues through his twelve-week internship, and he churns out a lot of great code. He primarily sticks to himself. He doesn't interact with any other interns or any other teams. He talks to team members when they approach him, but he rarely initiates a conversation. His twelve weeks go quickly, and by the time he gets to the end of it, Ted may be a stronger technician, but he's still the same guy he was when he arrived. What's wrong with this picture?

Well, conventional wisdom is flat-out wrong. To ignore your weaknesses is to stay in your comfort zone. And staying in your comfort zone is a recipe for being average. This is exactly what Ted did. He never put himself out there. He didn't stretch himself beyond his current level of shyness. Here's the deal. You don't have to completely reinvent yourself and become someone you're not. You have a certain set of skills that you're good at and you enjoy, and you most certainly should spend time becoming more of an expert in those areas. However, the only way you can grow is if you stretch yourself outside of your comfort zone.

Ted would have achieved much more success in his

internship if he had been more aware of his weaknesses ahead of time and made it a point to look for opportunities to stretch himself. He could have offered to lead a session with other software engineers on what Ted's current college curriculum covers. He could have asked for opportunities to speak at department meetings on a topic he's passionate about. Would this have been terrifying for Ted? Most likely, yes. That's the point. You can go through the motions and blend in with the crowd, or you can find ways to grow. The choice is yours.

Fast forward five years. Where is Ted now? The *stay* in your comfort zone Ted is still doing the same job with very little career advancement. The step *outside* of your comfort zone Ted is the technical lead of his department with many more advancement opportunities in his future. When you step outside of your comfort zone, you'll realize you're capable of much more than you previously believed.

Don't get me wrong here—I realize you can't be great at everything. You will have certain areas where you excel and others in which you're mediocre. And that's fine. The goal is to take on (and ask for) assignments, tasks, and projects that are just beyond your skill level. This is how you stretch yourself.

Grab your workbook and fill out the strengths and weaknesses section under Chapter 1. Be honest with yourself about your weaknesses. If it's helpful, consult your personality test results to come up with your lists. You'll reference this assessment throughout your internship, so make it clear where you struggle. If you want a great resource about an extreme way of stepping outside of your comfort zone, check out *Rejection Proof* by Jia Jiang.

## WHY ARE YOU DOING THIS?

Why are you looking for an internship? If your reason is simply so you can add it to your resume, then you're wasting your time. Seriously! Resume building is not as important as it used to be.

If you're only doing an internship because someone told you to, it's time to think long and hard about your motives and intentions. It's fine if someone else prodded you to get you to the point where you realized an internship was important, but if you're going to undertake an internship, you'll need to understand its true value. Showing up and going through the motions is not going to provide you with the growth necessary to springboard you into a great career.

Think about how you answered the question regarding your future career at the beginning of this chapter. Where do you want to be in five years? This is a very common question during the internship interview process. By considering it now, you'll be ready with an honest and passionate response. With this in mind, think about how your internship can help you get where you want to be five years from now. What should you try to accomplish during your short internship? Of course, you need to provide value to the organization that hires you as an intern, but for now, focus on what you personally want to get out of your internship. Record your response in your workbook.

You now have a purpose behind your internship. Nice work! Making it through Chapter 1 is already an achievement because many people won't take this step seriously. But you're here, and you're taking it seriously, so well done. Next we're going to take a brief look at fine-tuning your resume and cover letter. I'm sure your school offers help for this as well that you should be taking advantage of; however, I'll be providing you insights from a hiring manager's perspective. Even if you've already landed an internship, I'd encourage you to go ahead and read all the way through this book. You might just pick up a valuable golden nugget of info during the next few chapters—with topics that go beyond landing an internship.

## TAKE ACTION

❑ Access your workbook from https://ryanglick.com/
   intern-resources.
❑ Fill out your career objective in your workbook.
❑ Identify your strengths and weaknesses, and add them to
   your workbook.
❑ Think about and record your reason for getting an
   internship.

# CHAPTER 2

# Fine-Tune Your Resume and Cover Letter

*The richest people in the world look for
and build networks; everyone else looks for work.*
—Robert Kiyosaki, author and businessman

The best way to put together a solid resume is by learning from the mistakes of others. To do this, we're going to look at many of the common mistakes I've seen as a hiring manager over the years. Whenever I saw one of these gaffs, it'd make my spidey senses tingle. It signaled a red flag (or at least a yellow flag) that something wasn't quite right with the candidate. Does the candidate not pay attention to detail? Does the candidate lack motivation? Is the candidate mature enough for the position? These are all thoughts that would go through my head when reviewing a resume and seeing these mistakes.

Do such mistakes always mean your resume will get tossed in the garbage? No, not necessarily. But a sloppy resume won't land you any interviews, so why risk it? And don't worry. All of these mistakes are all easily avoidable if you follow the advice I've outlined below.

## COMMON RESUME AND COVER LETTER MISTAKES

**1. Spelling Errors.** Spelling mistakes may not seem like the end of the world, but they make you look careless. To help avoid spelling mistakes, always run spell check on your resume. This should be done automatically by the tool you're using to create your resume; however, some of Microsoft Word's advanced settings might mean spell check doesn't work as you'd expect. In addition to this, grammar recommendations are often inaccurate, too. So beware. And don't blame the tool for your own oversight. Also, remember that spell check doesn't always detect the meaning of a word in the context of a sentence. Spell check could see the word "the" and think it's fine when the word really should have been "them." These are things you'll have to look for when reviewing your resume manually.

When reviewing your own resume, print it out and review it physically with a pen. Don't proofread it on the screen. I get it—you may be wondering who uses a printer anymore? Many studies have shown that we catch more mistakes when looking at our work on physical paper than when looking at the computer screen.

One other tip for you: read your resume out loud. This will help you identify any sentences that just don't sound quite right. You can always have a family member or a friend read it out loud to you, so you can simply observe how it sounds. Trust me. You'll find things to change when you do this.

If you want to take your proofreading a step further, and you're willing to spend a little money, hire a professional proofreader. It's actually not very expensive to do this. There are countless services online where you can pay to have a professional editor look over your resume. If you don't want to hire a professional, at least get a second and maybe third set of eyes to look over your resume. This could be a family member or friend or really anybody who is willing to give you fifteen minutes of their time to help you out.

Finally, something is bound to slip past you. So don't fret. Analysis paralysis is real, and there's no need to spend hours and hours proofreading a one-page resume. Spend some quality time proofing, and go through the checklist I've provided in the workbook. After this, you'll be good to go.

**2. Formatting Issues.** You've just finished up your resume, and it looks great. You click the button and submit it to apply for an internship. The hiring manager on the other end opens up your resume file, and it looks all garbled—or at least it doesn't look like the version you saw on your screen. This happens quite often, and it gives a shaky first impression.

To avoid this, always convert your resume into a text-searchable PDF. Unless the application process requires that you send a Word document or some other specific file format, stick with PDF. If you're unsure how, you can search online and easily find out how to convert your document to a text-searchable PDF. There are some internships (and jobs in general) that will require you to copy and paste your resume into a text box. I understand why some companies do this with the vast number of people who apply for their positions, but it's still lame. And it's not a great sign that the company will do anything other than leverage artificial intelligence to analyze the keywords in your resume. In these cases, you don't really have a choice as to how you'll submit your file. However, when you do have a choice, always send your resume as a searchable PDF.

**3. Including Meaningless Info.** If you're not able to relate a piece of information to the internship you're applying for, then don't include that information on your resume. If you were a babysitter when you were fourteen, that's not relevant to an internship in software development. Sure, you could say that it taught you responsibilities at a young age, but that's a stretch. That was almost ten years ago, after all.

Make sure everything you include in your resume makes a strong case for why you are a good fit for the position. You're selling your skills to the company. You need to put yourself in the hiring manager's shoes and ask yourself who *you* would hire for the position. What attributes would that person need to possess? Don't distract the hiring manager's attention, or waste their time, with meaningless details.

In addition to this, keep things current. What have you been doing recently? This would be a good time to showcase some of the side projects that you've done outside of school or any formal job. Simply add a section on your resume labeled "Projects," and add your personal project details there. Companies, even the Fortune 500s, love to see self-starters and innovators who showcase their personal projects.

In the information technology world, I've frequently seen resumes that include experience at restaurants or home improvement stores. Any work experience is better than nothing, yet the inclusion of these jobs also made me wonder if they had any real IT experience. When no IT experience is included on a resume, I question what these individuals were doing in their free time. Were they playing video games? Were they out partying? Were they sleeping all day? Not that any of these things are inherently bad in moderation; however, there are so many educational things these candidates could have been doing to grow their skills and prepare them for a serious career. So as you can imagine, when I only see jobs unrelated to the position they're applying for, it leaves me with a lot of questions and doubts. If you don't have any work experience related to the position you're applying for, then it's okay to include your unrelated work experience on your resume. However, it'll be important to also include some of your personal technology projects to strengthen your resume and to prove your potential.

Keep your message on point and entirely related to the position you're applying for. And yes, this may mean you have two or three different resumes that you create for different types of positions. This is completely normal and necessary in many cases. Let's look at a couple examples of how you could have two different resumes when applying for internship positions.

- **Resume 1: Your resume for a software developer internship.** You'll include details around software development work you've done in the past—including any work history and personal projects. Your technical skills will be the focal point of this resume. That said, it'll still be important to include your soft skills.
- **Resume 2: Your resume for a technical business analyst internship.** You'll include the same work history and personal projects as on your software developer-focused resume; however, your description about each position will differ. Instead of focusing first on the software development skills, you'll focus more on how you used your soft skills in each position. Your soft skills will be the focal point of this resume, and your technical skills will be secondary.

**4. Lying About Your Skills and Experiences.** Very rarely is a college student going to be an *expert* at anything. This doesn't mean that it's impossible, but it's rare because the average college student simply hasn't been alive long enough to learn from various life and work experiences. So don't label yourself an expert or advanced for certain skills you list on your resume. Of course, if you're legitimately an expert at something, and you can prove it, then it's fine to say so. Just be prepared to explain your definition of "expert." When deciding your skill level, don't compare yourself to other college students; compare yourself to people who are already working in the industry. So if you say you're an expert at something, this means that you are essentially as good at that thing as a senior team member who has been in the workforce for many years. Ultimately, *just be honest.*

In addition to this, don't include buzzwords on your resume unless you're truly experienced with them and can demonstrate your level of experience. If you once heard some technology buzzword in the seventh lecture of some class during your fresh-man year in school, well... you shouldn't include that on your resume.

It's far too common for applicants to stuff as many buzz-words into their resume as possible to look more experienced. Don't be this person. You can be confident in your skills and still be honest. If you really want to stuff a bunch of buzzwords and industry lingo into your resume, you can spend time outside of class studying these topics to boost your knowledge. Better to be smart than sound smart.

**5. Using a Weird Email Address.** This one may surprise you, but it no longer surprises me. If you've been using a "funny" or "clever" email address since middle school or high school, it's time to create a new email address. Over the years, I've seen some email addresses that have made me scratch my head. Unless an email address is extremely vulgar, it won't necessarily keep me from interviewing someone; however, it can raise a caution flag before the interview even starts.

Back when I was in high school, a good friend of mine had the fantastic email address of BlondeTomCruise@aol.com *(note: he no longer has this email address).* This may be a great email address to have for a modeling internship, or it could drive intrigue for a creative internship, but not so much for a position in business or IT. If you have a goofy email address, get a new one.

**6. Broken Links.** If you include a QR code or a link on your resume to showcase a project portfolio or a personal website, make sure these links work. It shows a lack of attention to detail if you include a link that goes nowhere or is no longer active.

To avoid this, be sure you test every link. If you use any QR codes, print out your resume and scan each code to ensure they work as expected.

## HOW TO MAKE YOUR COVER LETTER STAND OUT

Not all internships require that you write a cover letter, but you should always create one and include it if the submission platform allows. A cover letter gives you a much better opportunity to stand out to a potential employer than a resume alone. When you write a cover letter, customize it for every position. Don't use a generic cover letter that you send in for every internship you're applying for. Sure, it will take some time to customize your cover letter for each internship application; however, it will show the company that you took the time to research them. Most applicants don't do this. They take the path of least resistance and shotgun out their resume to as many companies as possible as quickly as possible. Don't be like most people. You *need* to customize each cover letter to stand out and show why you're a good fit at that company.

Here are a few things to consider when you customize your cover letter:

- Be confident, but don't be egotistical.
- Keep it concise—don't write a novel.
- Address the hiring manager by name, if possible.
- Fully research the company and the company's industry to offer up specifics as to how you would be a good fit for the position.
- Discuss reasons why you want to work for the company—what is it about the company's culture or mission that hits home with you?
- Your cover letter is like a sales letter. You're selling yourself. You need to persuade the company to get you to the next step in the process. You're not trying to get a job with the cover letter; you're trying to get an interview.

## A SALES LETTER FORMULA FOR YOUR COVER LETTER

The following is a formula that is commonly used to write successful sales letters, and it dates back to the early 1900s. Although he's not the originator of this framework, one of the best copywriters of all time, Gary Halbert, references the framework in his June 26, 1984, letter from his famous "The Boron Letters" series. Countless copywriters have discussed this formula since then.

You don't necessarily need to follow this formula; however, I'd encourage you to study how it works. Once you understand the framework's power and how it influences the person who reads it, it'll guide you to writing a persuasive cover letter.

**The Framework**: AIDA, which stands for Attention, Interest, Desire, Action, is a great rule of thumb to follow when you set out to write any type of sales copy—print ads, sales letters, radio ads, or your cover letter. Let's dive into each of the four parts of the AIDA framework—in the order you'll use them:

1. **Attention**: Start out your cover letter by getting the attention of the hiring manager. You have a short amount of time to do this, just a sentence or two. Do something to stand out from the crowd. Be creative, but relevant, and try different approaches until you find one that works.

2. **Interest**: Now that you have the hiring manager's attention, it's time to keep them interested. You can capture the interest of the hiring manager by making your message personal. For example, you could mention some of the pain points the hiring manager experiences when searching for and interviewing intern candidates.

3. **Desire**: After the hiring manager is interested, you now need to build up their desire to interview you. To do this, you need to describe the benefits you will provide the company if they bring you in for an interview. Desire is created by tapping into the hiring manager's emotions through highlighting benefits, not features;

that is, don't talk about the drill, talk about the hole the drill will make. In terms of the skills you can offer a company, don't talk about your experience; talk about the results you'll provide. This is a great time to use a few bullet points that demonstrate your knowledge of the company and how your skills can benefit them.

4. **Action**: Lastly, you must explicitly tell the hiring manager what action to take. This is often where many people will get timid, put their tail between their legs, and end without a call to action (CTA). Don't do that! Don't be timid—you need to direct the hiring manager to schedule an interview. With this said, make sure you do this in a professional and polite way or you'll come across as arrogant and rude. For example, you could end your cover letter with: "I'd appreciate an opportunity to interview for this internship position at Company X. I look forward to hearing back from you with the next steps."

Again, you don't need to follow this formula exactly for your cover letter, but you should analyze all four steps to fully understand how they work. Then you can utilize the concepts to help write a persuasive cover letter that will get the hiring manager to schedule an interview with you.

## TAKE ACTION

❑ Review the sample resume and cover letter included on the resources page for this book (https://ryanglick.com/intern-resources).

❑ Check your resume and cover letter for the six common mistakes discussed in this chapter.

❑ Spend time reviewing the AIDA formula to better understand how it can improve your cover letter.

# CHAPTER 3

# Find the Right Internship for You

*Obstacles don't have to stop you. If you run into a wall, don't turn around and give up. Figure out how to climb it, go through it, or work around it.* —Michael Jordan, businessman and former American basketball player

Now that you better understand your goals and objectives for getting a technology internship, you're ready to find one that will make your career goals a reality. If you had no other choice but to accept an internship that didn't gel with your overall goals, I would tell you to take it for the general experience alone. But that doesn't have to be the case. There are plenty of internship options out there. Finding an ideal internship is well within your reach.

## WHEN TO START LOOKING FOR AN INTERNSHIP

It's best to start your internship search one year prior to when you'll be ready to begin. Most internships occur over a 10- to 12-week period in the summer months. In order to best position yourself for a summer internship, you should start your search at the start of the fall semester. For internships that occur during the spring semester, you should start your search when the spring semester ends. And so on.

## PAID VERSUS UNPAID INTERNSHIPS

Money is important. It's not evil. Money is necessary to support a family, support social issues, and live a great life. Yet it's not the most important consideration when choosing an internship. In fact, there are many unpaid internships that can be more beneficial to your future success than paid internships. How much do you care if you get paid (or not) for your internship? This is something you have to determine for yourself. I don't believe you should be concerned with how much an internship is going to pay you; I believe you need to focus on other tangibles and intangibles. Money is essentially infinite—you can always earn more. Your time on this earth is finite. Don't waste a summer internship trading time for money. Your summer internship needs to be much more than a paycheck.

If your financial situation precludes you from considering an unpaid internship, you still have another option. You could consider taking on another job during your internship. This may be painful for the duration of the internship; however, it will provide you with the financial means to make an unpaid internship an option. And when it's over, the lasting benefits of your experience will be worth much more than an internship paycheck.

## BE TRUE TO YOUR WORD

When it comes to accepting an internship offer, be true to your word. If you're going to apply, then commit! Don't back out unless something legitimate is stopping you (such as a sick family member in another city). Not honoring your commitment is a bad way to start off your career, and it most certainly will burn a bridge with the company you back out on.

You're going to have multiple internship opportunities at the same time, so you need to be prepared for a situation in which your ideal internship company is dragging its feet while your second choice is quick to offer you a position.

What should you do? If you tell your second option you need time to think about it, they may end up pulling the offer and giving it to another candidate. And nothing guarantees that your first choice will even offer you a position. I know there are many schools of thought as to whether you should back out of an offer for something "better," but I believe in keeping your word. If you can't keep your word, or you really don't want a position in the first place, then decline the offer and hold out for something better.

## DRUG TESTS AND BACKGROUND CHECKS

I'm not here to judge what constitutes a drug and whether they should be legal or illegal. What I am here to tell you is that you need to understand that your future internship employer most likely will have you take a drug test. They will also likely do a background check on you. I don't need to dwell much more on what this means, so I'll leave you with this: if you're asked about any arrests during the application process, be honest. And if you're into recreational drugs, well, an internship may not the right path for you until you change your habits.

## WHERE TO FIND INTERNSHIP OPENINGS

There are many resources you can use to find internship options. Here are a few:

- College career fairs
- Your college advisor
- The careers pages on websites of businesses you're interested in
- Your connections/network
- Job placement sites (i.e., Monster, Indeed, ZipRecruiter, LinkedIn, etc.)
- Social media (search for keywords such as #internship, #InternOpenings, and other combinations)

You can also reach out directly to hiring managers via email, social media, direct messages, etc., but don't be annoying. You must use this option in the right way or it will push the hiring manager away. This is essentially a cold email or cold reach-out, and it is very difficult to do correctly. If the individual is active on social media, begin following them and engaging with their posts (like, comment, and share). This will allow you to get to know them on a deeper level, and it will also make them aware of your interest. Then, after you've engaged with them for a few weeks, reach out and ask them about internship openings at their organization. It's important to realize that your engagement on social media must be genuine. If you aren't being genuine, it will show, and you'll be ignored. If they aren't on social media, and you're only able to connect with them via email, then be upfront in your message. Let them know you're interested in an internship opening, explain why you're interested *in that specific company*, and then ask if it'd be okay to send your resume.

## YOUR COLLEGE'S CAREER CENTER

You're paying a lot of money to go to your college or university. Take advantage of the resources that you have available right at your fingertips. Many colleges have career centers where you can get hands-on assistance during your internship or employment search. So in addition to completing your own internship research online, don't forget to check out your school's career services department.

## GET YOUR RESUME INTO THE RIGHT HANDS

You won't always have the option to send your resume directly to a hiring manager but when possible, that is the goal. Although the human resources (HR) group within most organizations plays a role in the hiring process, the hiring manager is responsible for making the final decision. *HR doesn't hire candidates; a hiring manager does.* This is important to know because the application process within the majority of larger organizations begins with HR. This means HR has the ability to filter resumes and cover letters without any hiring managers seeing them. This could be a problem for you, because it means there's a chance the hiring manager will never even see your application, resume, or cover letter. What can do you do to turn the odds in your favor? There are three things you should consider to increase the odds of getting your resume seen by the right people.

**Understand the Level of Competition:** If you want to intern at Google, you're going to be competing with thousands of other candidates. The good news? Not all internships will have hundreds (or thousands) of candidates applying for them. And your odds are much higher if you apply for an intern position with a smaller local organization.

One way to improve your chances of landing a highly competitive internship is to determine if anyone in your network has a connection within the organization where you want to intern. Knowing a company's popularity is all-important because your approach (and options) will differ depending on the level of competition for an internship.

**Capitalize on Your Career Fairs:** Always treat career fairs like you would an interview. Plan out what companies you want to visit ahead of time, and create your resume and cover letter for each company as you would if you applied for an internship on a company's website. You can't show up to a career fair and just hand out the same resume to every company without preparing. This is a recipe for mediocrity.

Have a plan. Determine the order in which you'll visit each company's booth. Create a customized resume and cover letter for each company you plan to visit, and get to the career fair right when it starts. By doing this, you'll be more prepared than 95 percent of all other students. Trust me. I've worked at many career fair booths over the years, and students are rarely prepared. The vast majority simply wing it. And I'm sure it wouldn't surprise you, but many students even show up looking like they are still hungover from a long night out at the bars—which reminds me: don't go out drinking the night before a career fair. Get some sleep, and show up refreshed and ready for many great discussions.

When you talk to the company representatives at each booth, be sure to ask a lot of questions about the company, detailed questions that make it clear you know what the company does. Also, ask the employees what they like about working for the company. Find out what exactly they do there. You never know—the person you're talking to could end up being a hiring manager. If so, jackpot!

If you have enough time and if there's more than one person at a booth, it's a good idea to talk to multiple people to get different perspectives. Some companies will do on-site interviews after the career fair. This is why it's so important to bring your A-game to each and every booth at each and every career fair you attend. If you shine, you may get an interview sooner than you expected. Just remember, if you prepare for career fairs, you will stand out—in a great way! Be a member of the 5 percent, not the 95 percent.

**Leverage Your Connections**: Often the most effective way to get your resume noticed is through any prior connections you may have. Whether it's someone you know directly or someone you know through two, three, four degrees of separation, look for people who can help. Whether it's family, friends, friends of friends, uncles, aunts, cousins, or even college professors, these connections can introduce you to hiring managers at organizations where you want to intern. You may not think you have an existing network, but trust me, you do. So use it!

Fair warning: because you're going to rely on your network a lot over your career, make sure you're also helpful to others who reach out to you. If things end up being too one-sided (with you asking for help and never providing help), you'll burn bridges, and your reputation will be tarnished. This will quickly shrink your network.

Over the years, many people have approached me directly about friends, colleagues, or family members expressing interest in open internship positions. In every case, I've asked them to email me their resumes. This is perfect for the candidates. Their resumes are going to be sent directly to me, and they even have a chance to research me and customize the cover letters with my name.

The normal mindset of a college student looking for an internship is to blast their resume to the world. They apply for any internship they can find, so their resumes and cover letters are generic. This is the path of least resistance. If you want to get ordinary results, then you can go down this ordinary path. If you want successful results, then you need to make your resume and cover letter stand out, and leverage your connections when possible.

## TAKE ACTION

- ❑ In your workbook, list ten internship options that you're interested in.
- ❑ Rank your internship options in the order of your level of interest, with 1 being your top choice and 10 being your last choice.
- ❑ In your workbook, list five career fairs you're interested in attending.

# CHAPTER 4

# Apply for Your Ideal Internships

*There are risks and costs to action. But they are far*
*less than the long range risks of comfortable inaction.*
—John F. Kennedy, thirty-fifth U.S. president

With your list of ten internship options now in place, it's time for you to take action. You're going to break your list down into bite-sized chunks to make it easier to manage. This will also reduce the likelihood of you feeling overwhelmed by such a large list. The plan is to split your top-ten list into five groups of two, starting with your highest-ranked internships.

## MAKE YOUR LIST MANAGEABLE

Starting with your top two internship opportunities, take the following steps:

1. Research each of these internship opportunities in detail.
2. Apply for each position following the strategies discussed earlier in this book.
3. After you're done with the top two, start back at step one for the positions that you ranked 3–4. Do the same

type of research, and apply for the positions. Continue until you've researched and applied for all positions.

## RESEARCH YOUR INTERNSHIP OPPORTUNITIES

At this point in the process, your research will be used to write an effective and meaningful cover letter. When you land an interview, you'll spend more time researching the company and the individuals you will be interviewing with. For now, here are a few questions to think about as you spend time exploring the company's website, social media profile pages, and news articles.

**What is their company culture like, and would you fit well into it?** The word "culture" has many interpretations, but for now just focus on how the company operates. Do they have a relaxed office environment? Do they appear to have fun? Do they enjoy what they do? Is their motto something along the lines of "Work hard, play hard?" Do they encourage personal growth? Or do they seem to work their young employees 65+ hours per week? Whatever their culture, you need to determine if it matches what you're looking for.

**How can you provide value to the company?** Remember, this isn't a one-sided transaction. Sure, you have your own goals and objectives for an internship, but what value will you provide to the company? Put yourself in the hiring manager's shoes. The hiring manager is generally looking for someone who is hard working, able to quickly pick-up new technologies, a self-starter who needs little direction, and interested in working full-time at the company following an internship. Any candidate who meets or exceeds these expectations will be valuable to an organization. Think about your skills and qualities that may provide value to the company.

**Have you ever worked on a project in the past (i.e., in college, on your own, or in another internship) that closely relates to the position you're applying for?** If so, this will provide a solid one-liner to include in your cover letter or somewhere else in the application process. If not, no worries at all. Although, I'd encourage you to spend some time brainstorming and experimenting with personal project ideas to bolster your resume and cover letter.

**Do you know anybody who has interned at this company in the past?** If your answer to this question is yes, then you need to talk to that person. This will help you fast-track the research process and may give you a foot in the door.

## APPLY FOR YOUR INTERNSHIPS

Each internship is going to have its own application process. You need to follow the application process instructions *exactly*. Many internship candidates are cut immediately after applying because they weren't able to follow simple instructions. If you're asked to provide a document with one-inch margins, 11-point Times New Roman font, saved in Microsoft Word 2003 format, then this is exactly what you need to do. I have no idea why anyone would ask you to do this—save the file in such an old format—but you get the point. Follow the application instructions, even if they don't make sense to you. And don't forget to send that cover letter you worked so hard to perfect!

## TAKE ACTION

❑ Go through your top-ten list of internships you identified in Chapter 3, and apply for each one following the exact instructions provided by the company.

❑ While you wait for interviews, go back to Chapter 3 and create a second top-ten list. This will really be your 11-20 list of internship options. Start this additional list immediately after you've finished applying for all of your 1-10 internship options. You're never guaranteed an interview, so you need to put in the effort to keep searching for internship options.

# CHAPTER 5

# Nail Your Interviews

*The most powerful way to convince the interviewer that you can do the job is to show how much you already know about the industry, the company, and the products / services of the company. In other words, enchant the interviewer with how much you already know.* —Guy Kawasaki, author, speaker, and venture capitalist

The interview is not the time for you to learn about the company you're interviewing with. You should have done that work long in advance and reviewed it right before the interview. The minute you display a lack of knowledge about the company and industry is when the interviewer(s) will begin to question your dedication.

I'd say around 80 percent of the interns I've interviewed over the years have shown up for interviews with no idea what my company does. At most, they've had a vague understanding that we "do something with technology." This raises an immediate red flag, and it's rather frustrating, to be honest. The other 20 percent have at least a basic understanding of the company and industry. The top 5 percent have come into the interview having clearly researched the company and the industry. They may not know exactly what they'll be doing in the position (which is completely understandable—how *would* they?), but they understand how the company works and what it's known for. Let me tell you, from the position of the hiring manager, this is very impressive. You'd think this should be the norm, but far from it. Your objective in the interview is to showcase your knowledge in order to stand out. The only way you can do this is through thorough preparation.

## RESEARCH, RESEARCH, RESEARCH

Take another look at the quote from Guy Kawasaki at the beginning of this chapter. The only way to have this kind of knowledge about a company, industry, or products and services a company offers is to do *a lot of* research. This doesn't mean doing a ten-minute Google search. You need to put in the effort to build a foundational understanding. This is not going to be a quick-and-easy task. It's going to take some time and commitment. But it will all be worth it when you show up to an interview fully prepared and confident.

You should have already done some basic research to assist you with writing your cover letter. Use that as your starting point for completing additional research ahead of your interview. While you're doing your research, jot down questions about things that truly interest you about the company. If you read about a decision the company made and you're wondering why that decision was made or what the outcome was, you can use this as a question in the interview. For instance, maybe the company merged with another company last year. What has this done to the company culture? Is the merger still in progress? Many things you read about can be turned into great interview talking points. Sure, maybe your interviewer won't know the answers to some of your questions. But they might, and your interview then becomes an opportunity to learn more about the company. Either way, it will show that you spent time researching the company, and this will put you ahead of the majority of other candidates.

It's quite possible that your research will uncover multiple reasons you might not want to work for a company. Ideally, you will find this information before you even apply for a position, but that won't always be the case. No worries, though. Write these reasons down as questions to ask during your interview to confirm your understanding. You're not going to cancel your interview because of some information you found while researching. Use this information to make the interview even more intentional and relevant. If you don't end up liking the company after the interview, you can respectfully decline any internship offer you may receive.

## REVIEW SAMPLE INTERVIEW QUESTIONS

IT interview questions will come from many different angles. You'll have more technical questions that will aim at finding out how much granular knowledge you have, and then you'll have questions focused on your soft skills—how well you interact with other people. Although your technical skills are important in the world of information technology, your soft skills are just as important, if not more so. I personally care more about soft skills, such as personality, than I do about how "smart" you are with technology—though of course I still expect candidates to have an aptitude to learn. For some sample interview questions that focus on soft skills, check out the resources page at https://ryanglick. com/intern-resources.

The list of interview questions I've provided does not include technical questions. Because there is such a wide variety of information technology intern positions out there, it would be impossible to provide a list that would be applicable to all such positions.

So you're going to need to do a little research on your own for this one. If you're interviewing for a software engineering position, look for sample software engineering technical interview questions. These will likely include questions around application design patterns and architecture, including real development problems. For instance, one of my go-to technical questions for candidates interviewing for a software engineering intern position is to have them write code on a whiteboard to reverse a string. The method takes in a string value, such as "rabbit," and it needs to output "tibbar." And no, they can't just do a string.reverse() call. I even allow candidates to use pseudocode to do this, although it's much more impressive if they're able to write legitimate code without any syntax errors.

Regardless of what type of intern position you're interviewing for, be sure to look for and study potential technical questions that might come up.

## MOCK INTERVIEWS

The best way to improve at interviewing is to…well, interview more. It doesn't have to be an interview for a real job, either. Mock interviews are a great way to gain experience and ease your nerves ahead of the real thing. You have many different options with mock interviews. You can reach out to your school's career services department to see if they offer mock interviews—generally they do. Or you can also head over to https://ryanglick.com/intern-coaching and see the options I have available through my one-on-one coaching program.

Regardless of who you complete your mock interviews with, it's important to ensure you get a few in before you head to your first real interview.

## BE EARLY

I've had candidates show up several hours early (seriously), two minutes early, and several minutes late, and I've even had some who no-showed. There isn't a one-size-fits-all answer to how early you should arrive to an interview, but it's important that you do arrive early. This will reduce your stress levels, and it will also demonstrate your level of responsibility and commitment.

Arriving early to an interview doesn't mean you need to be sitting in the company lobby sixty minutes before your interview. Instead, you could arrive at the office building and sit in your car for several minutes before heading inside. This will give you more control over the situation and reduce the likelihood of bad traffic or some other unforeseen event throwing off your timing. I'd also encourage you to do a dry run to the location of your interview a few days ahead of time. This will make you familiar with the best route to take and give you an idea of the full timing. This way there will be no surprises on your first day.

## DRESS THE PART

This one is tricky. Every company has a different culture, and you need to get to know each business and dress accordingly. Always err on the side of dressing up versus dressing down. In many cases, this is going to mean wearing a nice suit. In other cases, a blazer or sport coat with dress pants or a professional skirt might be more appropriate. And for some Silicon Valley internships, this may mean strolling in with a t-shirt and jeans. Again, it really depends on the culture of the company you're interviewing with. You can always contact the hiring manager or your human resources contact to ask about the expected attire. In the world of IT, when in doubt, wear a nice suit.

Another thing to think about is how much you sweat. If you tend to sweat a lot, pay attention to the color and material of the clothes you'll be wearing. You don't want to wear a color or fabric that you'll sweat right through. Generally, darker colors do a good job of hiding sweat.

I sweat a lot, so I can relate to this. I once bought a nice new shirt without a second thought for the material. I wore it (for the first time) to a large business meeting, and the room was really warm. About halfway through the meeting I realized I was starting to sweat right through my shirt in the armpit area. Yikes! I kept my arms down tight for the remainder of the meeting, and I was uncomfortable. I've never worn that shirt in a similar business setting since, and I now pay attention to the types of clothes I wear.

You can't control the temperature of the room you'll be interviewing in, so control what you can: the clothes you wear. You can even test your suit (or whatever you plan to wear to your interview) by wearing it in a warm room. Be smart with this if you're overly sensitive to heat. The goal is to put yourself in a situation in which you can test how well your interview clothes handle sweat prior to the actual interview. It wouldn't be the end of the world to sweat through a shirt, but you want to be comfortable and not worry about something like sweat during your interview.

## GET ENOUGH SLEEP

Just as it's a bad idea to stay up late cramming for a test, it's also a bad idea to stay up late cramming for an interview. Getting plenty of sleep is the most important thing you can do the night before your interview. If you want to gain a better understanding of how sleep impacts performance, check out *Peak Performance: Elevate Your Game, Avoid Burnout, and Thrive with the New Science of Success* by Brad Stulberg and Steve Magness. It covers not only sleep, but also many other factors that contribute to success. It's a great book to add to your reading list.

## DON'T FORGET THESE THINGS

In all of the craziness leading up to an interview, it can be easy to forget something. Here are a few of the items I recommend you bring along to your interview:

- Notebook and pen
- List of interview questions to ask
- Extra resumes in case your interviewers forget to bring copies to the interview

- A bottle of water—you're going to be doing a lot of talking, so be prepared with some water to keep your throat from drying out

I'd suggest you make your own checklist and include the items above plus any additional items you find necessary, such as personal grooming items, Kleenex, or breath mints.

## BE CONFIDENT AND RELAX

Your first interaction with the interviewer is going to be a handshake. I know you've heard this countless times, but it can't be overemphasized: you need to start things off with a firm handshake. You don't want to lead things off with a limp-fish handshake. You may think it's goofy, but practice your handshake with someone else. Practice until you have your handshake down. The goal isn't to break someone's hand; the goal is to show confidence. A firm handshake (while making eye contact) accomplishes this.

This next one's much easier said than done: you need to focus on remaining calm and relaxed ahead of (and during) your interview. What's the worst thing that could happen? You struggle through the interview and don't get the job? Big deal! You'll have other interviews. So don't feel like your back is against the wall. View your interview as an opportunity with no downside.

**Think About A Prior Success**. It can really help to think about a time in your past when you excelled at something. Maybe you won a competition or aced a test. Think about that ahead of your interview while you're in the waiting room. Know that you are capable of being successful.

**Practice Deep Breathing**. Another thing that will help you relax is taking a few deep breaths before you walk in the room. You may see this as hokey, but give it a chance. It works. Look for a guided breathing app to make it easier to follow through. Or, if you don't want to mess with an app, you can simply take deep breaths in through your nose, and then release your breaths out of your mouth. This has a calming effect and can decrease an elevated heart rate.

**Slow Down**. When nervous, most people talk really fast. When you're aware of this, you can consciously focus on slowing your speech down. By doing so, you'll also help settle any anxious feelings you may have.

## TELL STORIES

Boring people are forgotten. If you regurgitate bullet points from your resume throughout your interview, you'll be boring. And you'll be forgotten. To improve engagement and bring more entertainment to your interview, you need to be prepared to tell stories. Stories stick in people's minds. When I think back to all of the intern interviews I've conducted over the years, the candidates who told stories are the ones I remember. Whether the story is about something that happened to you during childhood that is relevant to the position, a class project you've worked on, or a situation you came across during a high school or college job, interesting stories sell.

Because this isn't a book on storytelling, I'm not going to dive into the weeds on how to tell a great story. There are many existing resources out there to help. For instance, I'd recommend *Do You Talk Funny?* by David Nihill.

## THANK THE INTERVIEWERS

After the interview is complete, you're not quite done. Of course, thank the interviewers for the opportunity before you leave the interview room. But it doesn't stop there. You also need to send a personal thank-you email to each of the individuals who interviewed you. If you're unsure of their email addresses, ask your contact at the company to forward your thank-you along to them. Ideally, though, you'll be able to send a custom message to each person.

A thank-you email is great, but a handwritten thank-you letter is even better. If the hiring decision is expected to happen quickly, then the hiring manager may not receive your thank-you card before the decision is made. This is fine. You should still mail it. However, in this case, you'll also want to send a thank-you email. It won't hurt to send both.

## TAKE ACTION

- ❑ Thoroughly research the company prior to your interview.
- ❑ Practice answering the sample soft skill interview questions included in the Chapter 5 section of the resource page (https://ryanglick.com/intern-resources).
- ❑ Find technical interview questions specific to your field and spend time studying them.
- ❑ Create your own interview checklist to ensure you don't forget anything important the day of.
- ❑ Following your interview, send thank-you emails and physical cards to all interviewers.

# CHAPTER 6

# You Landed an Internship—
# Celebrate It!

*Character cannot be developed in ease and quiet. Only
through experience of trial and suffering can the soul be
strengthened, ambition inspired, and success achieved.*
—Helen Keller, American author and lecturer

We are often way too hard on ourselves. We focus so much attention on the things that don't go as planned, and we give very little attention to our successes. When you land an internship (notice I said "when," not "if"), be sure to take some time to celebrate. This doesn't mean go out and get crazy. Simply take some time to reflect on how much effort it took for you to get to this point. Think about all of the calculated action you had to take to *earn* this position. There are a number of ways for you to celebrate. Go to a movie. Go get some ice cream. Take a night off of your hard work to get some drinks with your best friends or have a nice dinner with someone special in your life.

With this said, don't rest on your laurels. Stay hungry, and continue to work your butt off during your internship. In Part 2, we're going to discuss how to prep for and make the most out of your internship.

## TAKE ACTION

❑ Spend some time reflecting on your successes.
❑ Do something fun to celebrate your new internship.

# PART 2:

# During Your Internship

In this part of the book, we're going to focus on all of the considerations and action items you need to keep in mind during your internship. It's not enough to just show up to your internship and go through the motions. You must take explicit actions, such as:

- Properly communicating with your manager before your internship
- Keeping a journal to track your successes and failures during your internship
- Using your mentor to help you through challenges
- Sending thank-you notes to your team members, human resources, and the hiring manager

# CHAPTER 7

# Prep for The Start of Your Internship

*I believe that people make their own luck by great preparation and good strategy.* —Jack Canfield, author and entrepreneur

Your internship is right around the corner, so all you need to do now is just show up, right? Not quite. You may be wondering what kind of prep work you need to do before starting your internship, and this is a very good question. Who is responsible for making that prep work happen—the employer or you? Unless your soon-to-be employer gave you a list of things you need to do before starting your internship, then technically there is nothing you need to do. Yet the reason you're reading this book is because you aren't merely interested in what you *need* to do. You're interested in taking steps that will help you excel. When the majority of people will simply show up to their internships without thinking twice about any of what we're about to cover, you'll have a great opportunity to shine. So even if you aren't officially required to do any prep work, there are steps you can take to ensure you show up to your internship well prepared and with a purpose.

## REACH OUT TO YOUR MANAGER

Your internship manager has a lot on their mind, so they may not always get in touch ahead of your internship. I know that I've fallen short on many occasions over the years, and sometimes I failed to reach out to my soon-to-be interns. This is why you, as the intern, need to be proactive and get in contact with your manager.

If you don't have a manager assigned to you yet, then you can call or email your human resources contact directly.

There are two primary goals for reaching out to your manager:

1. **Gain more specifics on how to prepare**. You should ask for their insights on anything they would recommend to help you prepare for your internship. Are there any technologies you should spend time studying? Is there a specific vendor product you'll be working with that you should research? Really, you're looking for anything and everything that you can add to your preparation list. Use your hiring manager's feedback to write down three specific things to learn more about prior to the start of your internship.

2. **Keep an open line of communication**. This will show that you're engaged with this internship opportunity and that you care. If you get hired in October for a summer internship the following year, this means it will be a full seven months before you show up for day one. This is a long time for radio silence. You need to fill this void with the right amount of communication.

I suggest checking in on a monthly basis. Then, when you get to one week away, reach out one more time. You don't want to be annoying or take up too much of their time, so keep your email communication brief. You can share something new or interesting that happened in one of your classes or on a personal project. It will also be a good idea to ask how your manager and the team are doing. If you know they're working on a certain project, then be thoughtful and reference that project. Show that you've been thinking about your prior conversations. This will help you keep a pulse on things. Plus, when you show this level of ambition, motivation, and communication, it may even persuade your manager to give you more responsibilities during your internship.

Set yourself reminders to reach out to your manager once a month. If you leave it up to your memory, you'll most likely forget. I use a calendar for recurring tasks and reminders, and I strongly suggest you do the same.

## DESIGN A MORNING ROUTINE

You're about to step into the business world—possibly for the first time. The way to be successful is by creating a predictable routine. You need to identify all of the things you want to get done each morning and then schedule it all out.

For example, here is what my daily routine looks like:

- **5:30 a.m.:** Wake-up to my Apple Watch buzzing
- **5:35 a.m.–5:45 a.m.:** Practice meditation and visualization
- **5:45 a.m.–5:55 a.m.:** Write in my daily journal
- **5:55 a.m.–6:15 a.m.:** Read a nonfiction, entrepreneurial book
- **6:20 a.m.–7:20 a.m.:** Exercise
- **7:20 a.m.–7:50 a.m.:** Breakfast
- **7:50 a.m.–8:30 a.m.:** Get ready for work
- **8:30 a.m.:** Head to the office

A routine will bring consistency and predictability to each and every morning. The routine I've outlined above is how I operate during the weekdays as well as on the weekends. As you prepare for your internship, you need your own morning routine. Work backward from the time you will need to be at work each day, and then fill in anything you want to get done before work. By doing this, you are in control of your day, and your day is not controlling you.

*The Miracle Morning* by Hal Elrod is largely responsible for overhauling my mornings. I used to sleep in as late as possible before I had to get ready for work. This always made me feel rushed and out of control. If I wanted to be to work by 8:00 a.m., I would wake up at 7:00 or even 7:30 and scramble to get ready in twenty minutes. This was not ideal, and it started my days off terribly. Once I implemented my own Miracle Morning routine, I was much more in control and confident heading into work. Plus, I knew that with my morning routine, I was accomplishing more before going to work than the majority of other people were accomplishing throughout their entire day. This gave me a great feeling of pride.

In your workbook, fill out your own morning routine. What do you want to accomplish every morning to set yourself up for success?

## PRACTICE YOUR ROUTE TO WORK

It's time to go through a practice commute (or practice public transit journey) into your soon-to-be office. I know this seems unnecessary (or like overkill), but it will help ease your mind ahead of your first day as an intern. The last thing you want is some surprise road construction or a route that isn't as fast as Google Maps told you it was.

Now, if you don't live in the same city where you'll be interning, then this may not be possible until you get really close to day one of your internship. If you're doing things correctly, you should get to the city of your internship a few days ahead of day one. Assuming you do this, you'll still be able to go through a practice transit. Here's what you're going to do:

1.  Map out your trip using Google Maps (or your favorite navigation app).

2. Go through the planned route on a business day *at the exact same time* you'll be commuting to work. Don't go through a practice commute in the evening or on a weekend (unless that's when you'll be commuting for your internship).

3. Make mental notes along the way of any possible travel bottlenecks or changes you should make to your route.

4. Once you're back home, update your morning routine to account for the travel time you measured during your practice commute. During the first week, give yourself a 100 percent buffer on your travel time until things are comfortable. For example, if your commute is thirty minutes, then you should allow an additional thirty minutes—so sixty minutes for your commute time. After the first week, you should still give yourself a little time buffer for your commute.

## GO ABOVE AND BEYOND EXPECTATIONS WITH SELF-IMPROVEMENT

Earlier in this chapter, we discussed reaching out to your manager on a recurring basis before your internship begins. The information that they provided to you should now be put to use. There aren't many better ways to impress your soon-to-be employer than by stepping into your internship fully prepared. You won't need hand-holding or several weeks to grasp the basics. Don't get me wrong here. You won't know everything—far from it. That's one of the purposes of the internship after all: to learn. However, by preparing, you'll be the best version of yourself, and you'll likely be well ahead of prior interns.

It's completely up to you how you prepare. For instance, you can use training websites—such as PluralSight, Udemy, or LinkedIn Learning—to learn more about specific technical topics. You could find a local tutor to train you. Or you could go the free route and search out training and educational videos on

YouTube or Vimeo. Find a platform that is geared toward your preferred way to learn.

## PREPARE YOUR JOURNAL

Writing down and documenting your thoughts every day is a scientifically proven method for personal growth and mental clarity. Have you ever used a journal before? If not, no worries. It's simple. Even if you've had a negative experience with a journal in the past, I'd encourage you to be open to it—give it another try. It really works.

The objective of your internship journal is to document the process and ensure you stay on track toward achieving the personal goals and objectives that you outlined in Chapter 1. It will also serve as a record to show you how much you've grown throughout your internship.

Here's how you're going to use your journal (which you'll find on the resources page at https://ryanglick.com/intern-resources):

- Print out the journal, ideally printing double-sided to save paper. Physically writing in your journal is important because you process things better when you write than when you type. This is the advantage of printing the journal and writing in it by hand, but if you prefer to maintain a digital journal, I've provided you with that option as well.
- Review the sample journal entry to better understand how you'll use the journal each day.

We'll talk more about how you're going to use all of your valuable journal insights in Chapter 9. For now, it's time to start your internship!

## TAKE ACTION

- ❏ Set a calendar reminder to communicate with your manager on a monthly basis.
- ❏ Set a calendar reminder to communicate with your manager one week prior to the start of your internship.
- ❏ Determine the three most important topics that you need to learn more about before your internship begins.
- ❏ Plan and write down your morning routine, including your commute time.
- ❏ Select a platform for training, and then begin to consume as much information as possible about the three topics you identified.
- ❏ Prepare your (printed or digital) internship journal before your first day on the job.

# CHAPTER 8

# Making the Most of Your Internship

*Be humble. Be hungry. And always be the hardest worker in the room.* —Dwayne Johnson, American actor, producer, and entrepreneur

I'm sure the wait has felt like an eternity, but it's finally time to start your internship. You should feel good about all the preparation you've done up to this point. Your internship mission should be clear, and your motivation to succeed should be at an all-time high. Now it's time for us to talk about considerations for your time in the office. Whether it's a ten-week internship, a twelve-week internship, or a semester-long internship, the topics we're going to cover in this chapter will help make your internship a success. You've put a lot of time and energy into getting to this position, so let's keep your momentum going.

## UTILIZE YOUR MENTOR

Most companies will assign mentors for their interns. If you aren't assigned a mentor, you should request a primary point of contact. And if you aren't given a primary point of contact, then you'll be using your manager as your mentor. Even if this person isn't officially called a "mentor," we're going to refer to them as one here. Your mentor will give you the inside scoop on how things are done within the organization. Remember, your mentor isn't necessarily on the same career path as you, so be careful with their advice. You'll run into some mentors who are not motivated by their careers, so their advice could take you in a direction you don't want to go. As long as you keep this in mind, you can respectfully listen to all advice and then take action accordingly.

It's important to schedule a thirty-minute one-on-one meeting with your mentor when you start your internship. If your mentor doesn't schedule this, be proactive and schedule the discussion yourself. During this meeting, express your goals for the internship and also express your interest in helping the team in any way possible. Be careful with this conversation. You're not trying to step right in and be a leader, so make it clear that you're looking for your mentor's advice and guidance to ensure you're doing things correctly. Many people have said it before me, but as the saying goes, you must learn to follow before you can lead. Just make sure you're following the right person.

What if you're assigned a bad mentor? Well, this happens. You can't guarantee that you'll get a mentor who actually cares about your success. If you happen to get a mentor who clearly couldn't care less about you, then you have a few options.

- If your mentor is never available, you should mention this to your manager. They will be able to tell you if there is a specific team member you can talk to when your primary mentor is unavailable.
- Reach out directly to other team members if you need additional assistance. You don't necessarily need to pull your manager into every conversation. As I've said before, be proactive.
- If your mentor is trying to sabotage you (which is highly unlikely), you need to talk to your manager about this to get direction.

## BE CONSISTENT AND ON TIME

You may think that people won't notice if you're a few minutes late here and there, but they will. Even if your team members or manager aren't explicitly looking for you, it's just something that people see. Because you want to be the best team member—and best person—you can be, you need to be consistent. This includes being consistent with your work performance and being consistent with the time you arrive at the office. If you're inconsistent, you will not only let your team and the company you're working for down; you will also let yourself down.

By this time you should have already confirmed your work hours, so be sure you stick to the schedule. Even if you are stepping into an office environment with a flexible work schedule, it's still a good idea to be consistent with your work hours. And if there is a day where you're going to be late, you need to communicate this in the appropriate way. If your manager wants a phone call or a text message, then you need to make that call or send that text. Don't show up late without telling your manager.

## OBSERVE SUCCESSFUL PEOPLE

You'll quickly learn who the successful people are on your team and throughout the organization. By successful, I don't mean the people who are the highest on the career ladder. I'm talking about the people who others respect. People who have real influence and persuasion within the organization. This doesn't always come from having the most elite title. When you find these people, pay attention to them. Look for certain traits that they possess. Respect must be earned, so what have these people done to earn it? Do they work hard? Do they devote quality time helping others on the team? Are they great listeners? Do they articulate complex solutions in a way that is easy to understand? Have they been in the industry for a long time and have a lot of experience?

The goal of observing successful people is to better understand how you can become successful yourself. This is a great habit for you to develop in life in general. Always be observing successful people.

## SAY YES TO OPPORTUNITIES

As an intern, you've been hired to do a job, so you can't be picky about what you work on. In addition, you should want to take on each and every opportunity that comes your way. Even if it doesn't fit in with your internship goals and objectives, you never know what will transpire from each project or task. So as new opportunities are presented from your mentor or your hiring manager, happily take them on. Sure, you won't always be excited to do tasks that seem meaningless or tedious, but you still need to do the work to the best of your ability. No slacking or complaining.

## BE POSITIVE

You're going to be interacting with many different personality types. Some personalities will be great to work with, while others may drain your energy. No matter how negative others around you are, you need to stay positive. Your mindset influences the quality of work you produce, and a negative mindset can sink you quickly.

If you can help it, avoid negative people in the workplace. Don't hang out with them. Don't congregate where they congregate. Don't go out to lunch with them. Find the positive people, and spend time with them.

This is true for your personal life as well. If you have friends, family members, or classmates who are negative all the time, you need to avoid them. I realize this is harsh to say about friends and family, but it's true. Negativity breeds negativity, and it's hard for anyone to stay positive in a negative setting. You don't have to be mean to these people; just spend less time with them. Find a new group of like-minded (and positive) people to spend time with.

The more successful and positive people you're around, the more successful and positive you'll become.

## AVOID OFFICE POLITICS, AND DON'T GOSSIP

As much as companies may not realize it, gossip and office politics run rampant in many workplaces. It can be easy to fall into the mob mentality and become a gossiper yourself if you spend time with others who gossip. Gossip and office politics can include disagreements with an organizational decision, discussing the personal life of someone in the organization, preferential treatment of a team member, and many other destructive behaviors and conversations. Essentially, if you're talking negatively about someone else—without that person being present—then you are gossiping. If you sense that gossip is taking place, leave the conversation. Just realize that gossip will happen, and you need to avoid it at all costs. And if you're trapped in a conversation that turns to gossip or office politics, never participate in the discussion.

## OWN YOUR MISTAKES

You're going to make mistakes. Even if you don't make a huge mistake during your internship, you'll make some big mistakes at some point in your career. Big mistakes and small, always own your mistakes and be honest about them. The sooner you can come clean and start finding a solution, the better. Let me share a quick story about a big mistake I made early on in my career.

It was six o'clock on a Saturday morning and I was reviewing some records following an overnight data update of millions of rows. My heart sank. The data was wrong! My heart started beating faster, and I tried to figure out what had gone wrong. I struggled to not panic. I wanted to leave the office and never go back. Instead, I continued to research the situation while the rest of the project was still moving along. The project stakeholders wanted an update from me, so I had to give them something. I had to own up to the mistake, and I let the project stakeholders know there was a problem and that I was looking into it. I quickly found the issue. It was a typo in my script. Ugh! I would now have to tell them that I made a mistake in my script, which would also tell them that I didn't test a script that was being used on a multimillion-dollar project. Yet that's what I did. I told the truth. I owned up to my mistakes, and I told them how I'd rectify the situation. I fixed the script and tested it, and then I spent another twelve hours correcting the data. The project was thrown slightly off schedule, but we hit our go-live date.

Although you'll make mistakes throughout your internship (and career), it's important that you don't make the same mistake twice. I can assure you that I never made a similar data update mistake throughout the rest of my career. If you make the same mistakes over and over again without learning and growing from them, then you won't have a job very long.

The bottom line is that mistakes happen, so be honest. Own your mistakes, and learn from them.

## BE ACCOUNTABLE TO YOURSELF

By reading this far into the book, you've taken the initiative to make your internship the most valuable experience possible. You still need to hold yourself accountable to fill out your journal *every single day.* Your journal is very powerful, but only if you use it. The insights you'll glean from your journal throughout your internship will help you grow tremendously. So don't skimp on your journaling. Seriously! Set a reminder every morning and every night to write in your internship journal. It can be the first thing you do when you wake up and the last thing you do before you fall asleep.

Although you need to hold yourself accountable, I'm also here to be your accountability partner and help you find success. You can join me (and other successful interns) on the inside and start receiving pep talks, technology career advice, and personal growth trends throughout the week. Join my insiders list by going to https://ryanglick.com/intern-insiders.

## LEARN DURING YOUR COMMUTE

How long is your commute to and from your internship each business day? Twenty minutes? Forty-five minutes? Sixty minutes? Two hours? However long it is, you can use your commute time to your advantage. Don't just listen to music or some pop culture or sports talk show. Instead, spend your time listening to podcasts and nonfiction audiobooks to help you grow personally and professionally.

Think how many books you could finish over the course of your internship. No joke, I believe you could average one book every week and a half. Of course, this depends on how long the books are, but you get the idea. How much could you learn during your commute alone? I listen to between 100 and 150 audiobooks every year. And this is all from my time spent commuting, walking, waiting, and so on. If you start doing this during your commute, it'll turn into a habit. What better habit can you think of forming in your life than that of self-education?

This is something that I started to do later in my career. I wish I had come across this idea much earlier in my life. Today, you'll find me with ear buds in constantly. I'm always trying to learn something new to help my own personal growth. I'll share my top fifteen books and top three podcasts in the last part of this book. These are a great place for you to start with your own personal growth journey.

## BEFORE YOUR INTERNSHIP ENDS

Toward the end of your internship, there are a few things you need to do. First, you'll more than likely have an exit interview scheduled with the human resources department or your hiring manager, or maybe both. If one isn't scheduled, request one. Heading into this exit interview, you need to ask yourself a few questions:

- Has your experience at Company X been positive?
- Would you be interested in working part time at Company X while you're in school (either remotely or physically in the location, if possible)?
- Would you want to intern at Company X again?
- Would you want to apply to work full time with Company X after you graduate?

If your responses to the questions above are mostly positive, then you're going to approach the exit interview in an active manner. Your goal will be to begin the process of applying for and locking in an internship for the next year or getting an inside track toward becoming a full-time team member. Or maybe your experience was positive, but you'd still prefer to look elsewhere for another internship or for full-time employment.

Whatever your preferred future employment path, don't close the door on Company X. You never know where things will end up, so you always want to keep doors open.

If you think you might want to intern again for Company X or apply for a full-time position, then ask the question during your exit interview. Ask about the application and hiring process and the timeline for a prior intern like yourself. Demonstrate and express interest in joining Company X. Realize that not every company that hires interns is interested in having those interns join full time or come back for another internship. Ideally, you did the appropriate amount of research up front and discovered this during the interview process.

Finally, ask your hiring manager if they would be willing to serve as a reference for you in the future. Ask in a way that leaves the door open to coming back to Company X. For instance, you would ask, "Would you be open to being a reference for me in the future if I don't end up getting a position here at Company

X full time?" More than likely, your hiring manager will agree to this.

## SEND A THANK-YOU MESSAGE

Before your email account with the company is deleted, send your team (and any other people you worked closely with during your internship) brief thank-you emails. The goal of the email is to thank your team members (and potentially others) for their help throughout the internship, and then provide them with your contact information. Providing them with your contact information is key here.

The team has been emailing your work email address for the entire internship, and most of the team has no idea what your personal email address is. You never know when someone on the team may want to reach out in the future, so make sure they can reach you if they want to. Don't send an email to the entire company; only send it to your close contacts.

Yes, the email is important, but a physically mailed thank-you card will mean a whole lot more than a thank-you email. So send both. The first thing you want to do when you are finished with your internship is send a handwritten thank-you card to your team as well as your manager. It can also be a good idea to send a card to your human resources contact. Be sure to make each card personal and share what you found to be most valuable about the experience. Again, this should be a physically mailed card, not an email. Receiving a handwritten thank-you card is very uncommon these days. I can count on one hand the number of times I've received such a thank-you card from one of my interns. Because this is so uncommon, it will make you stand out. Plus, it's the right thing to do to show your gratitude. Your team and manager just invested a lot of time and money into your personal growth, after all—be thankful.

## STAY CONNECTED

During your internship, you met a lot of people. You may have developed some friendships with other interns or team members. These connections will be important for you to maintain; however, there are other connections you need to think about as well. You also need to maintain contact with some of your professional connections. This will vary by internship but will usually include your hiring manager. It's critical that you send periodic messages to your internship manager to stay in touch. Just like you did prior to your internship starting, you can set a reminder to reach out every couple of months or so until you graduate. You don't want to be overbearing, but you do want to get in touch frequently enough to stay top of mind in case any opportunities come up in the future for which you'd be a great fit.

## TAKE ACTION

- ❑ If a mentor isn't assigned to you, request one.
- ❑ Schedule a thirty-minute one-on-one meeting with your mentor.
- ❑ Request (or schedule) weekly one-on-one checkpoint meetings with your hiring manager.
- ❑ Join other successful interns and subscribe to my insiders mailing list by going to https://ryanglick.com/intern-insiders.
- ❑ Subscribe to at least two educational podcasts, and start an Audible subscription (or to save money, use your library card along with the OverDrive mobile app to gain access to books and audiobooks).
- ❑ Ensure you have an exit interview scheduled with your hiring manager.
- ❑ Send your team (and other close contacts) brief thank-you emails that include your personal contact information.
- ❑ Send personal, handwritten thank-you cards to your team and your hiring manager for the internship opportunity.

☐ Identify all of the professional connections you made during your internship, and jot down their contact information in your workbook. You can also add your connections in the back of your internship journal.

☐ Schedule recurring reminders to stay in contact with your professional connections.

# PART 3:

# After Your Internship

In this part of the book, we're going to focus on all of the considerations and action items for immediately after your internship. Just because your internship is over doesn't mean you don't still have some work to do. If you truly want to become the best possible version of yourself, then you'll want to continue with this section, where we'll discuss:

- How to complete an internship retrospective to analyze your internship performance—including setting future action plans to improve

# CHAPTER 9

# Internship Retro

*If you know you are on the right track, if you have this inner knowledge, then nobody can turn you off... no matter what they say.* —Barbara McClintock, American scientist and cytogeneticist

As I'm sure you're aware, the term "retro" as it's used in this chapter title does not refer to fashion from the past. The definition of retro in the form we're using it here comes to us from the world of agile project management, where retro is short for retrospective.

A retrospective is an opportunity to identify the good and bad from your recent past and identify a plan for improving. What does this mean for your internship? Well, it will mean analyzing the internship that you recently completed and creating a plan to improve your future self. Before continuing, make sure you have enough time to effectively analyze the questions below and ten-plus weeks of your journal entries. I'd recommend carving out two hours (at least). A retro isn't just something to check off of your list. It's meant to provide you with tangible action items that you'll be able to build your future around. So don't skimp on this section.

Okay, assuming you have at least two hours right now to start your retro, let's dive in.

## REVIEW YOUR JOURNAL ENTRIES

Before you answer the three traditional retro questions discussed below, take a first pass at reading through your journal. During this first pass, there is no need to take notes or to thoroughly examine every word or phrase you wrote. Instead, read through your completed journal with an open mind, and feel good about what you've accomplished. It may take you a little bit to get through your notes from every single day, but read through it all.

Once you've gone through all pages with a first pass, you should have sparked many thoughts about what you experienced throughout your internship. Bearing these in mind, you can now continue with the retro questions.

## WHAT DID YOU DO WELL?

Think about this question for a minute: what did you do well during your internship? I'm sure you can think of many things. Go through your journal day by day, and then write down everything you feel you did well during your internship. Your journal notes should give you a lot of ideas, so read them in more detail during this pass. Write (or type) your thoughts in your internship workbook.

This is going to take some time. Don't be in a hurry. Think about how you performed with respect to some commonly admired traits in the business world:

- Did you communicate well with your team members and manager?
- Did you look for challenging opportunities?
- Did you work hard every single day?
- Did you do a good job of listening during meetings and one-on-one conversations with others?

- Did you offer up any suggestions or ideas to others?
- Did you always try to exceed the expectations when working with customers?

This list is for your eyes only, so feel free to brag. Now is not the time to be humble, but you should be honest with yourself. Once you've exhausted all of your thoughts related to what went well during your internship, move on to the next question.

## WHAT COULD YOU HAVE DONE BETTER?

Next, you need to look at the flip side of the last question. What could you have done better during your internship? Where did you falter? It's okay to have messed up during your internship. We all make mistakes. And trust me, this isn't something that stops after your internship. Everybody fails continually throughout life. That's how we grow. The purpose of answering this question is not to highlight your failures but to give yourself some ideas on where you can grow. Now, just as you did with the last question, go through your journal day by day, and make a note in your internship workbook of all the things that you could have done better. As before, be honest with yourself. Don't be afraid to hold yourself accountable.

Once you've exhausted all of your thoughts related to what you could have done better during your internship, move on to the last question.

## WHAT WILL YOU DO TO IMPROVE GOING FORWARD?

You've now gone through your journal multiple times. You've identified both the things you did well and the areas where you could have done better. You've been completely honest with yourself throughout this process. Now it's time to create a plan for personal and professional growth. Before completing this section, realize that you can't be great at everything. That's not the goal here. You're not trying to fix every weakness you may have. The goal is to prioritize and tackle the top three areas for you to improve.

Using your workbook, list ten areas you've identified from your internship where you could improve. Don't focus only on areas where you fell short; think about where you excelled, too. For example, let's say that you did a great job communicating with your team members during your internship, and your manager gave you this praise in your exit interview. If this was the case, then communication would most certainly be in your "What did you do well?" list. Yet you can still improve your communication. Dig deeper and think about a specific area of communication where you could improve. Maybe it's your written communication, your in-person verbal communication, or your body language. As before, the goal here is not to pick on weaknesses exclusively and improve them—the goal is also to take your strengths and make them even stronger.

After you've documented your list of ten areas for improvement, number the list from 1 to 10 in order of how meaningful a change in that particular area would be to your growth. Let's say that you missed a couple of deadlines during your internship because you couldn't figure out some issue. Instead of asking a team member or your manager for help, you were proud and wanted to figure it out yourself before anyone found out. So the issue dragged on, and this led to you missing your timelines. This is an example of letting your ego get in the way. For the previous example of communication, maybe you received positive feedback about how well you communicated with your team members during your internship, but you also realize you need to improve your listening skills during conversations. If you try to prioritize both communication and ego on your list, which should be ranked higher?

This is where you need to analyze how big of an impact improving each area would have on your overall growth. If you improve your listening skills, what will this mean for your personal growth? How about if you improve your ego? There is no clear-cut answer here. It will be different for every person. For me, getting my ego in check would have a much bigger impact on my success than would improving my listening skills—although both are extremely important, and they often go hand in hand. I would then rank ego as number one and listening skills as number two. Remember, we're going to focus on your top three.

Okay, you understand the exercise now. Go ahead and finish up your top-ten list, and then label them 1 through 10 in the ranking column on your worksheet.

## CREATE YOUR SELF-IMPROVEMENT PLAN

With your top-ten list of personal growth areas in front of you, use the ranking column to identify your top three. Then, rewrite (or type) your top three in the area provided in your internship workbook.

You're now going to use the next three sections of your workbook to create a plan for each of your top three areas for improvement. For each area, identify five actions you can take to improve in that area. Let's look at a quick example, and then we'll set you free to work on your top three list.

We'll use ego for this example. Here are possible action items you could write if ego was one of your improvement areas:

1. Listen before I speak in group settings.
2. Openly admit when I make mistakes, and never try to cover mistakes up or pass blame onto others.
3. Remember not to take it personally when my ideas are challenged by others.
4. Refrain from talking about other people when they aren't around.
5. Always do what's in the best interest of the project, company, or greater good rather than what's in my own best interest.

With a list like this in place, you would have specific areas to focus on to improve your ego.

Once you have a list of five action items for each of your top three improvement areas, it's time for one final step. You're going to spend one month focusing on each of your top three, starting with number one. During the next month, take a minute every day to look at your five action items for the highest-priority improvement area. You can do this by writing the action items down on sticky notes and placing them around your home or in your car, or you can simply review them in your journal. It's important that you review them on a daily basis, though, to keep them top of mind.

When you get to the end of one month, reflect on whether you've made progress. If you haven't made any progress, then you're going to continue working on the same improvement area for the next month. Otherwise, you're ready to move on to the second item on your list.

You now have a formula for identifying and improving specific areas of your personal and professional life. Even when you complete your three months of improvement (one improvement area per month), you should always look for specific areas where you can grow. I'd recommend you go back to your top ten list and work on the remaining seven improvement areas you documented. Ultimately, you should never stop learning and improving yourself.

## CONTINUE TO USE RETROS

Don't let this be the only time you reflect on your past. You should use retros frequently to make sure you're on the right track personally and professionally. You don't need to complete retros on a weekly basis or even a biweekly basis. I'd suggest a monthly or quarterly frequency for your personal retros. Simply throw a recurring meeting on your personal calendar, and go through your retro questions. You should block off an hour or two to give yourself enough time to fully reflect. You can change the three questions slightly to better align with your personal life:

- What has been going well in your life?
- What could you be doing better in your life?
- What changes can you make to improve your life?

## TAKE ACTION

☐ Complete your internship retro using your Internship Mastery workbook.

☐ Set a recurring monthly or quarterly reminder on your calendar to complete personal retros.

# PART 4:

# Accelerate Your Growth

While I was writing this book, I thought about several of the challenges I ran into as a college student and a new graduate. I made a lot of mistakes early on, and it took me a while to recover. This is why I decided to add this last part of the book. Within these final sections, I'll share some books and podcasts that will help you continue your personal growth and find success. In addition, you'll learn:

- How to avoid making the same financial mistakes I made
- Why going above and beyond for customers is so important
- If creating a personal brand is right for you

# CHAPTER 10

# How to Avoid the Same Money Mistakes I Made

*There is scarcely anything that drags a person down like debt.*
—P.T. Barnum, American showman and businessman

I was sitting in my dorm room with a few buddies, finalizing our plans for a trip out west to go skiing in Colorado. I was in college now, and the freedom was real. We were about to book a nice house in Vail, and we were going to split it among several of us. It was at this time I dug into the mail to retrieve a few of the credit card offers I had recently received. These credit cards would provide me with immediate spending power. But which one should I choose: 0 percent APR for six months, nine months, or twelve months? A $5,000 limit, a $10,000 limit, or even a $15,000 limit?

I eventually applied for two credit cards and was immediately approved. I didn't think twice about putting money on the cards. All I had to do was make the minimum payment, which was not much money at all. I wasn't even thinking about paying off the credit card in full. I'd take care of that in the future, I thought.

## THE SPENDING STARTED

I paid for the entire Vail house rental on my credit card, and then I had everybody else pay me in cash. I didn't use that cash to pay off the card, though. I used it for spending money. Plus, I needed skis, boots, and all new snow gear. No problem. I just put those on my credit card as well. The first card was quickly approaching its limit. So I started using the second card. I bought myself a computer, DVDs, CDs, all of the latest gadgets, and many other things I didn't truly need.

Before I knew it, both credit cards were nearly maxed out, and I was struggling to make the minimum payments. It felt terrible. The crazy thing is that my parents were still paying for my cell phone, my food, and half of my school, yet I still found things to put on my credit card and had very little of my own money left over to pay my bills. Whenever I'd get my student loan money, I'd use it to buy some more time on my credit cards by paying the card balances down.

By the time I graduated, I couldn't keep up with the credit cards anymore. I had increased my credit limits multiple times to maintain my level of spending. I was working a job making very little money, and the job wasn't helping me financially at all. It really didn't matter how much money I made, though. I was good at blowing it all.

I couldn't take it anymore. It was time to talk to my parents about the mess I had gotten myself into. They were shocked. They had no idea I had built up such a balance on my credit cards over the last four years. My credit card balances totaled over $20,000, and I was drowning. After I agreed to cancel my credit cards, my dad helped me out by cosigning a loan to pay off the cards. This debt didn't disappear, but I felt like I could breathe for the first time in a couple of years.

## THE SPENDING CONTINUED

Unfortunately, I didn't learn my lesson. I was back at "keeping up with the Joneses" in no time flat. Here I sat with over $20,000 in credit card debt and over $18,000 in student loan debt, but over the next couple of years, the spending continued. It may not have all been on a credit card, but I still found a way to leverage lines of credit to make purchases.

- Wedding loan: $7,500
- Fitness equipment: $2,500
- Car transmission: $3,500
- Lasik procedure for my wife: $3,000
- New car: $17,500
- Another new car: $15,000
- An expensive cat (don't even get me started): $2,500

Factoring in my wife's student loans, we now had over $100,000 in debt. This doesn't even take into account the fact that we had just purchased a new house that was more than what we should have spent. We bought the house back in 2007, just before the bubble burst and home values dropped. We financed the house at 100 percent (of course), and this put us in another bad spot. The mortgage, homeowner's insurance, and taxes stretched us thin.

## CHANGING MY WAYS

The company I was working for at the time had a great program that covered the majority of my grad school costs. Because of this, I didn't *need* to take out any student loans for school. However, I still had a plan for those student loans. The plan was to start my debt recovery process by taking out the maximum possible student loan amount and use it to consolidate my debt. As I received my student loan disbursements each semester, I would use the money to pay off my existing (higher-interest) debt. I ended up with over $50,000 in graduate school student loans that I used to pay off much of my other debt, and this simplified my payback plan at a lower interest rate.

In hindsight, this was a terrible idea. All this did was move money around. It didn't decrease my debt burden.

## PAYING MY DEBT DOWN

It was quite simple: to pay my debt down, I needed to spend less money than I made each month. The money I had left over would then go toward my debt payments. The more I had in excess revenue, the faster I could pay down the debt. So I turned to Dave Ramsey and his concept of the snowball plan. I ignored interest rates and paid as much as possible on the smallest loan. At this time, I had the following debt to pay off:

- Car loan 1: $11,825
- Car loan 2: $14,514
- My wife's undergraduate loan: $9,142
- My undergraduate loan: $12,996
- My graduate school loan: $51,822.81
- This brought my total debt to $100,299.81. Ugh.

## MY FIRST BUDGET

In order to have money left over at the end of the month to pay down my debt, I had to set a budget. This was the first time in my life I was going to take control of my spending. Previously, if I wanted something, I just went and bought it. Now, all purchases had to fit into my budget.

I'm not going to talk about how to create a budget here because there are hundreds, possibly thousands, of books on budgeting out there already. What I will say is that going from no budget to a very tight budget was hard. It took a full commitment from both my wife and me to stick to the budget. The cool thing is that it actually worked.

At the end of each month, we had more revenue than

expenses, and we were able to put that excess income toward our debt. The process wasn't perfect, and I faltered on occasion, but we maintained this budget until all of our debt was paid off—the undergrad student loan debt, the cars, and the graduate school student loan debt. We finally had no debt remaining, with the exception of our mortgage. It was an amazing feeling, and we kept it that way going forward.

## DON'T BE SHORT-SIGHTED LIKE I WAS

You'll hear the excuses all the time: "YOLO" (you only live once), or "you never know how long you have on this earth." These phrases are championed by people who spend, spend, spend. Don't be this short-sighted. Sure, you only live once, but what happens if you live to be 80, 90, or 100 years old? By being irresponsible today for some experiences or material possessions, you'll eliminate all control over your own future.

I believe that credit cards are fine as long as you can control your spending. Once I was able to get control over my budget and spending, I once again had a couple of credit cards that I used on a regular basis. It's all about self-control, being responsible, and sticking to your budget.

The reason I shared this story with you is to illustrate just how quickly things can get out of control with debt. What started out as a harmless purchase of a few material possessions for a ski trip quickly turned into a habit of debt. This habit controlled my life, and it could have been so much worse. I'm thankful for having a great family support structure around me because without that, who knows where I would have ended up. It may not have been such a happy and positive learning experience.

## TAKE ACTION
- ❑ Get a book on budgeting.
- ❑ Create a budget to control your spending.

# CHAPTER 11

# Fifteen Books I Wish I'd Known About When I Graduated from College

*Formal education will make you a living; self-education will make you a fortune.* —Jim Rohn, American entrepreneur and motivational speaker

Full disclosure: not all of the books mentioned in this section were even written when I graduated college. However, I didn't want to limit the list to only books released prior to May of 2004. So I've included my top fifteen book recommendations to date. These books have changed my life, and I'm confident that they will also change your life.

One piece of advice before we dive into the list: if you pick up the audiobooks, you don't have to listen to every book at normal speed. Most audiobooks are read at a slow pace by the author or the hired voice actor, so speed things up to 1.25x or 1.5x to bring the speed to a more natural conversation cadence. You won't miss out on any important nuggets, but you'll get through the books faster. This same advice holds true for many of the podcasts you listen to (which we'll cover in the next chapter).

Most public libraries offer free use of an app called

OverDrive. This app gives you access to many popular audio-book and e-book titles. If you don't have room in your budget for a service such as Audible or for buying the physical books, it's worth checking out OverDrive.

## BOOKS FOR PERSONAL GROWTH

### Influence and Persuasion:

1. *Influence: The Psychology of Persuasion* by Robert B. Cialdini, Ph.D.
2. *How to Win Friends and Influence People* by Dale Carnegie

### Entrepreneurship and General Business:

3. *The 80/20 Principle* by Richard Koch
4. *Unscripted* by MJ DeMarco

### Productivity:

5. *The ONE Thing* by Jay Papasan and Gary Keller
6. *The Miracle Morning* by Hal Elrod
7. *The Power of Habit* by Charles Duhigg
8. *Peak Performance* by Steve Magness and Brad Stulberg

### Financial Management:

9. *Rich Dad, Poor Dad* by Robert T. Kiyosaki

### Mindfulness:

10. *Think and Grow Rich* by Napoleon Hill
11. *Lead the Field* by Earl Nightingale
12. *The Four Agreements* by Don Miguel Ruiz
13. *Man's Search for Meaning* by Viktor E. Frankl
14. *As a Man Thinketh* by James Allen
15. *The Magic of Thinking BIG* by David J. Schwartz, Ph.D.

## TAKE ACTION

- ❑ Buy (or check out from the library) at least one book from the list above.
- ❑ Work through this list of books, and let me know your thoughts on each title—you can email me at ryan@ryan-glick.com.
- ❑ Begin to explore new book titles, and set a goal to read at least one new book each month.
- ❑ Create a habit of reading (or listening to an audiobook) *every single day.*

# CHAPTER 12

# Three Podcasts That Will Make You Smarter and Increase Your Personal Growth

*Anyone who stops learning is old, whether at twenty or eighty. Anyone who keeps learning stays young. The greatest thing in life it to keep your mind young.* —Henry Ford, businessman

Okay, the chapter title is a little misleading. You won't become smarter just by listening to these podcasts. You must take the time to implement the ideas that are presented during each episode. If you're willing to do that, podcasts are a great way to continue your personal growth journey. I personally mix in podcast episodes with audiobooks throughout my days. This keeps things fresh with more current event topics as well as new and classic book titles.

There are thousands of podcasts out there, so spend some time looking around for ones that fit your growth needs. The podcasts I shared below happen to be my current favorites—those that I've found the most valuable—but there are niche-specific podcasts you can look for as well. Maybe you want to find a podcast on a certain technology to help deepen your technical expertise. The ball is in your court here, but I highly encourage you to start with the three shows below.

If you find a show that provides you tremendous personal or professional value, I'd love to hear about it. Send me a note at ryan@ryanglick.com.

## PODCASTS FOR PERSONAL GROWTH

1. *The Smart Passive Income Online Business and Blogging Podcast* by Pat Flynn
2. *Ed Mylett Show* by Ed Mylett
3. *The MFCEO Project* by Andy Frisella

## TAKE ACTION

❑ Subscribe to at least one of the three podcasts in the list above.

❑ Search for and subscribe to at least one podcast that you find on your own.

❑ Listen to at least one podcast episode per week.

# CHAPTER 13

# My Two Cents

*The question isn't who is going to let me; it's who is going to stop me.* —Ayn Rand, Russian-American writer and philosopher

Since this is a book focused on making the most out of your internship, I didn't want to dilute this objective by dedicating a full chapter to any of the topics to come. Instead, my goal is to make you aware of these concepts and emphasize their importance to your success. So without further ado, here's my two cents on several different important topics.

## IMPROVE YOUR SOFT SKILLS

Let's face it: technology is changing. The hardcore technical skills of the past are becoming less and less necessary in the workplace. AI and machine learning are playing a big part in this. Although the need for technical experts is decreasing over time, soft skills are important across the board, regardless of the level of technical skills required at any given time. This is what will set you apart from others vying for the same job. With all of this said, I believe there will always be a need for elite technical experts, but the demand will be smaller as time goes on. Don't put your future in jeopardy by ignoring the importance of soft skills. You can start by focusing on the following: communication, collaboration and teamwork, problem solving, and leadership.

## MAKE EXCEPTIONAL SERVICE A HABIT

When I was growing up back in the 1980s and 1990s, my family and I would take frequent road trips all around the country. We'd hop in the full-size Gladiator van and hit the road. I remember my dad putting a $20 bill on the dash before we left our home in Iowa for each trip. His plan for that $20 bill? The first drive-through employee to tell him thank you would get the cash as a tip. We would occasionally hear "have a nice day," but that isn't the same as "thank you." Sadly, I don't ever remember us giving that $20 bill away.

Just think: if customer service was bad back then, it has only gotten worse over time. Customer service in the majority of businesses today is abysmal. Based on my own experiences, it is simply no longer a priority for most companies.

Why is this important for you? Because you have the opportunity to change this trend by placing a high importance on serving others to the best of your ability. Because service has gotten so bad, the bar is set low. It doesn't take much to give customers a great experience. Make it a goal of yours to *always* treat your customers with respect and tell them thank you. Not only will you stand out as a great team member; it's also the right thing to do.

## WORK-LIFE BALANCE IS *MOSTLY* A MYTH

If you study any great people of history, you'll realize how obsessed they were with their missions. Their lives were everything *but* balanced. You need to understand this and know what it takes to be great at any one thing. When I get my mind on something, my life becomes out of balance—and my wife lets me know about it.

In the business world today, you hear the words "work-life balance" championed over and over again. But what does this even mean? Some people will say it means spending forty hours in the office, and then leaving right when your forty hours are up so that you can go spend time on your "life." This is not a recipe for greatness. There are going to be times when your work will demand much more than forty hours. There will also be times when your home life will demand much more time than your work. Realize that if you strive for work-life balance in the traditional sense, it will be very difficult for you to become great. Things will never be evenly split 50/50.

## NICHE DOWN YOUR TECHNICAL SKILLS

In his book *Overdeliver*, Brian Kurtz says, "I want to stress the importance of choosing specialists over generalists…anyone who tells you they can handle all your marketing needs in their 'one-stop shop' is someone you should run away from fairly quickly." This quote is about marketing, but it is true of the technology world as well. It is difficult for generalists—also known as jacks-of-all-trades—to truly stand out from the crowd. It's not impossible, but it is difficult. I know because I was a jack-of-all-trades myself right out of school. Although my background was in software development, I found myself getting into a little bit of everything—from desktop support to server administration to business analysis to software engineering. I was all over the place. I'm sure I looked confused, and I was mediocre at a lot of things.

It's okay to dabble in a few different technologies while you're still figuring out what you enjoy. But once you figure out the technical area you want to focus on, go deep. This is how you'll grow and become highly sought-after in your industry.

## DAILY TASK LIST

It's easy for your days, weeks, and months to fly by. If you don't take control over each day, you are unlikely to achieve the success you're after. This lack of life direction is what's called aimlessly drifting. And trust me, drifting through life is not what you want.

To avoid drifting, you need to have a daily list of three critical tasks that will take you toward your goals in one of the eight pillars of life (family, health, wealth, education, career, spiritual, hobbies, and relationships). Every night before you go to bed, write out your three critical tasks for the next day. Your critical tasks need to be small enough in size that you can complete them within a single day. Look at the list throughout the day to stay on track.

If you continue to knock out your list day after day, you will find yourself fast-tracking toward a great future. This compound effect is nothing new that I'm inventing; it's been discussed in detail by many authors over the years. A few recent books on this topic include *The Compound Effect* by Darren Hardy, *Do A Day* by Bryan Falchuck, and *The ONE Thing* by Jay Papasan and Gary Keller, to name a few.

## NEVER STOP LEARNING

Most people graduate from college and think their learning is over. Who can blame them? They are done with school, so why would they think about continuing to learn? Well, believing that education ends at graduation is a false belief. It's important to continue to learn until the day we leave this earth. Life-long learning will not only help us find success in life, it will also keep our minds young.

Earlier, I shared a list of books and a few podcasts to check out. This is where your continued learning begins. From there, you can find other relevant ways to keep growing, such as training, seminars, conferences, and additional books and podcasts. Finally, look for an organized group of like-minded people that you can join. This is often referred to as a mastermind group—a concept made popular by Napoleon Hill in his book from the early 1900s titled *Think and Grow Rich*.

## PAY ATTENTION TO WHO YOU SPEND TIME WITH

Jim Rohn famously said, "You are the average of the five people you spend the most time with." Think about that for a minute. Who are the five people you currently spend the most time with? If you are surrounded by people from your past, friends you chose based on the person you used to be, these people may be holding you back unless they are also moving forward.

Sometimes it can be hard to cut ties with people you've known for a long time. But if you have toxic friendships or toxic people in your life in general, then it's time for you to consider finding new friends. Ask yourself these questions to determine if a friend or acquaintance is toxic. Do they drain your energy? Are they constantly negative? Do they question you as a person and not believe in you? Are they always bringing drama into your life? If you answered yes to any of these questions, then this person is toxic.

If you want to succeed, you need to surround yourself with people who have achieved the success you want to achieve yourself—or who are headed in that direction.

## FIND A MENTOR

Just as the internship mentor can be critical to your success as an intern, a life and career mentor can be crucial to the success of your life and career. Although you can look within your organization for a mentor, I'd highly encourage you to look elsewhere for someone successful to be your mentor. A mentor from outside of your organization will be an impartial sounding board when it comes to the topic of your career. And remember, mentorship can't be a one-sided transaction. What will your mentor get out of the arrangement? This may mean you paying them, or providing them with a skill set of yours at no cost. Tech skills are a valuable asset to offer mentors in exchange for their time.

Once you find a person who you want to be your mentor, reach out to them and present the idea. The person most likely has a busy schedule, so you need to respect their time. Be honest about what you hope to get out of the mentorship, and also tell this person what you can do for them in return.

You can always go at it alone, but remember this: even the most successful people in the world still use mentors. Having a mentor can speed up your learning process and allow you to run things past another individual who has likely experienced the same challenges.

## STUDY PERSUASION AND INFLUENCE

Every day you are influencing others and being influenced by others—even if you're not aware of it. This includes coworkers, children, spouses, salespeople, and virtually everyone you interact with on a regular basis. As such, you need to be proactive about studying the art and science behind persuasion and influence. Let me tell you a quick story about a time when influence was used against my wife and me (in an unethical way) when we were buying a car a few years back.

When we got to the first dealership, we knew exactly which car we wanted to look at. We told the salesperson (let's call him Joe) the vehicle we were interested in, and he started right in on his sales game. "We've had quite a few people call about that car already this morning. It sure seems popular." We didn't really think anything of that comment at the time, but it was Joe's subtle way to influence us by instilling a sense of scarcity and urgency. Hey, this car wasn't going to be around for long, so we'd better make a decision now.

After a test drive, we went to Joe's office. We told Joe that we liked the car, but we had another test drive scheduled at a dealership down the street. Joe knew that if he let us leave the building, we most likely would not be back. He told us to think it over for a few minutes, and then he left the office. My wife and I talked about it. That scarcity and urgency tactic from earlier was looming large in our minds. If we left, would the car sell to someone else before we got back?

About five minutes later, Joe came back into his office. Not more than a minute or two after him, another salesperson came walking into the room. This is when the real shadiness of their game started.

"Hey, Joe, I've got another couple out here interested in taking the 2007 Toyota Camry Hybrid for a test drive. Can you toss me the keys?"

Joe tossed over the keys to this other salesperson, and the other salesperson walked away. Joe told us not to worry, though. "You were the first ones here, so if you want the car, you have first dibs." This shifted the scarcity tactic into overdrive. Now, we felt we *had* to make a decision. If we left without buying the car, it would be gone for sure. After all, someone was there right then going for a test drive. Joe left the office again because he knew all he needed to do was let us talk ourselves into it with this scarcity on our minds. And he was right! Joe came back in a few minutes later, and we were ready to buy the car.

Was there truly someone else there ready to take a test drive, or was this simply a tactic? A car salesman friend of mine later confirmed it was in fact a common manipulation tactic. This is one reason that understanding the power of influence is so important. You can use influence in an ethical and mutually beneficial way to persuade others, and you can learn to protect yourself from the shady Joes of the world.

## NOBODY IS GOING TO DO THE WORK FOR YOU

I can still vividly remember sitting at my office desk back in June of 2008, thinking about where I wanted to go with my career. I believed that I was motivated. I knew I wanted to work my way up within the organization to become a strategic leader.

Great plan, right? Well, on the surface it seemed great, but I was blinded to a major internal problem. I thought, "I'm a hard worker, and I'm good at what I do. Why haven't I been promoted to a position of leadership yet?" Then a few months later came the moment I had been waiting for all along. My manager asked me to help him interview candidates for the team. He asked me to interview as if one of the candidates was "going to replace me." I became extremely motivated during the interview process. I did everything I could to ensure that the candidates had the qualities necessary to be successful at my position. This was my time to be promoted!

We found a really good candidate, and finished up the interview process. This candidate accepted a position on the team. I waited anxiously over the next couple of days for my boss to tell me about my promotion. Then he made an announcement to the team: one of our team members was retiring, and the new person would be replacing the retiring team member. No promotion for me!

I had been sitting around for the first two years at my organization waiting for someone else to promote me. I had become complacent, and I wasn't taking responsibility for my life. My problem was right in front of me the entire time.

From this point onward, I knew that I needed to better define my career goals and define the steps I would take to accomplish them. I took action, and I made a plan. I made my manager and others aware of my career goals and aspirations. Within a couple of years, I was promoted to a position of leadership. Without this experience, I'm not sure how long I would have stayed in that same role waiting and waiting for someone else to promote me. My *aha!* moment was realizing that *I'm* responsible for me.

My story illustrates how easy it is for us to settle and wait around for something good to happen to us. This problem extends far beyond our career goals. It's something we experience in all areas of our lives. Don't wait around expecting someone else to take action for you. You need to do the work and be responsible for yourself.

## DON'T WAIT FOR "SOMEDAY"

We've all fallen into the "someday" trap:

"Someday I'm going to be happy when I get that really nice car or that nice house."

"Someday I'm going to be happy when I get married or have kids or get the job of my dreams."

"Someday I'm going to get in shape."

"Someday everything will come together and work out as I planned."

The thing is, if you aren't happy right now, then you won't be happy in the future just because you achieve some goal. Chasing goals is a never-ending cycle.

Plus, as you continually look at the future, you'll be ignoring the present. And this is a problem. You need to focus on *now*. You can't change the past, and you can't control the future. The only thing you can control is what you do right now—at this very moment. Because this is the only control you have, be present and stop waiting for "someday" to make you happy. When you live in the present, you are more likely to enjoy the experience. However, when you are always focused on your past or your future, you're ignoring the journey. The only way you can truly be happy is when you're fully present in the *now*. So enjoy the present—it's all you have.

## STAY OUT OF THE RAT RACE

One of the most common things people struggle with financially—new grads and established professionals alike—is growing their expenses as their income grows. If a new grad makes $45,000 (after taxes) out of school, they will find a way to spend all $45,000. Then, when they receive a raise and start making $55,000 (after taxes), they'll increase their spending by $10,000. When a person falls into this trap, it doesn't matter how much money they make. They could be a doctor making $500,000 per year. If they spend $500,000 per year, it's the same as someone else making $50,000 and spending $50,000—they both end the year with $0. Sure, they may have more *stuff*, but they're not saving for the future. And even worse, what if the doctor makes $500,000 and spends $550,000? Then they have a major debt problem on their hands.

It can be tough to avoid this pitfall, but you must resist the need to impress other people with material possessions. Use the advice of Robert Kiyosaki in *Rich Dad, Poor Dad*, and instead, use your excess income to buy assets. Once the revenue generated from your assets is enough to pay for your "toys," then by all means, go buy your new Tesla or vacation home. For more information on buying assets, check out *Rich Dad, Poor Dad*.

## DON'T HAVE A VICTIM MENTALITY

Early on in my technology career, I was constantly playing the victim—although I didn't realize it at the time. I remember countless conversations with my managers about how I thought I was "too young" to be taken seriously by the executives in the company. I told myself this sort of thing over and over again. I told myself this so often that it became my reality. I was stuck. Maybe some older execs value tenure over performance, but not everyone thinks that way, and my assumptions were only holding me back.

Whatever you do, don't go through life with a victim mentality. You're not too young or old or short or tall or fat or skinny or any other attribute. You must operate with confidence and realize that any label you place on yourself can (and often will) become your reality.

Once I removed this limiting belief about my age, I quickly moved my way into a leadership role. The fact that I wasn't being promoted had nothing to do with my age. It was all in my head. In today's modern business environment, performance trumps tenure 99 times out of 100. Focus on giving your best, and there won't be anything stopping you from climbing your way to the top.

## UNDERSTAND THE POWER OF YOUR MIND

Not too long ago, I thought the power of the mind movement was a bunch of madness. I didn't believe in it at all. That all changed in 2010 when I was introduced to the concept by a family member. I'm now fully engaged and harness as much of my mental power as possible to help me succeed.

This book is not the place for a detailed discussion of the power of the mind, yet I want to encourage you to explore it on your own. There are many books and podcasts on the topic. A couple of classics that are often mentioned by successful businesspeople include: *As A Man Thinketh* by James Allen and *The Science Of Getting Rich* by Wallace Wattles. The books can be difficult to absorb during your first pass, so be sure to read (or listen) to them more than once. And don't stop there. Keep exploring the importance of meditation, visualization, and positive self-talk. I know these all may seem crazy at this point in your life. I get it. I was at the same spot. All I ask is that you give the idea a chance.

## IT'S EASIER TO TAKE RISKS EARLY ON

The older you get, the more complicated life becomes. There are many reasons for this: starting a family, becoming established in a career, and becoming comfortable with life in general. This doesn't seem so bad, right? Well, when you become comfortable, it's really hard to forego this comfort and take new risks. Because of this, if you have the inkling to try something new *now*, do it. Some examples of things to consider:

- Traveling (if it fits into your budget)
- Entrepreneurship
- Living in another city (or country)
- Trying a new career

With this said, you need to use your best judgment when you take risks in your own life. But even when you get older and your life becomes complicated, I'd still encourage you not to stop taking risks.

## NEVER GIVE UP

It was the year 2009, and a crazy friend of mine talked me into running a marathon. I wasn't just going to run "a" marathon, though. I set the goal of qualifying for and running the Boston Marathon. To do this, I signed up for the 2009 Chicago Marathon, and I trained intensely for over eighteen weeks. The day of the marathon finally arrived (October 11, 2009), and I was ready to go. I was on pace all the way through mile twenty-three. Then I "bonked" (also known as hitting a wall or running out of gas), and I walked most of miles twenty-five and twenty-six. Needless to say, I fell short of my goal and didn't qualify for the Boston Marathon.

In 2010, I was determined to achieve my goal and qualify for Boston. So I increased my training so I'd be in the best possible shape for the race. Race day in 2010 was hot, and I started cramping terribly around mile fifteen. I soon found myself in a medical tent getting assistance. After about thirty minutes of stretching and getting fluids, I was given an ultimatum: either get back on the course and finish running the race, or catch a ride to the finish line in their medic van. If I went with the first option, I would be continuing the race with no chance at all of qualifying for Boston. However, if I went with the second option,

I'd be giving up. I would have a DNF (did not finish) next to my name in the results.

It didn't take me long to decide what I was going to do. The medic confirmed there was little risk of further injuring myself by continuing, so I got myself back on the road and struggled through the remaining 11.2 miles. I didn't give up. I had worked hard, and I needed to finish to prove to myself how mentally and physically tough I was.

You're going to run into many challenges in your life and throughout your career. Never let any roadblocks cause you to give up. There is always a path forward. You just have to put in the hard work, and you will find it.

## YOUR HEALTH COMES FIRST

Without your health, nothing else matters. I find that if I'm not healthy, I can't take care of my family, play with my kids, build a successful business, and all the other things that are important to me. This is why health needs to come first, and why you need to prioritize your health as well. When you set your morning routine, exercise needs to be a part of the plan. But it doesn't stop there. You need to ensure you are eating the right food. I'm not a dietician, nutritionist, or a personal trainer, but I do place a high level of importance on exercise and nutrition in my own life.

The right amount of exercise and the right nutritional plan will be different for everybody, so you need to spend the time doing research to find what's right for you. Don't ignore it. Make health a top priority in your life.

## BUILD A PERSONAL BRAND

I believe that each and every person should take time to understand whether a personal brand will help them professionally. This includes you. Personal branding doesn't make sense for everybody; however, there are many of us who benefit from having a personal brand. Here are a few of the questions you should ask yourself to determine if personal branding is right for you.

Where do you want to take your career? The answer to this question will help you determine if branding makes any sense for you. Do you want to be one of the top thought leaders in your area of expertise? Or are you more focused on working your way up within a single organization? Neither path is inherently better than the other, but your choice will dictate whether you do anything with personal branding.

If you decide to focus on climbing the corporate ladder within a larger organization, personal branding may help; however, it doesn't need to be your highest priority. If you want to become known in your industry as one of the go-to people, then personal branding is a must—and it should be high on your list of things to focus on. So where do you want to end up? And remember, you can always pivot later and go in another direction. You may choose to work your way up within a single organization now and then change directions later, at which time a personal brand might be more helpful.

Today, there are an endless number of paths you can take to build a personal brand. Below are a few ideas to consider to help you build a strong personal brand:

- Speak at local technology club meetings or industry/trade conferences.
- Reach out to podcast hosts to be a guest on podcasts related to your industry and expertise.
- Create a personal website, and keep it up to date—ideally using your name for your domain name (i.e., ryanglick.com).
- Join online forums or groups related to your industry, and remain active. Help others by answering their questions and posting relevant and valuable content.
- Participate in conversations related to your industry on social media, and link all of your social profiles back to your personal branding website.

- Start an industry-specific blog (or vlog), and regularly post valuable content.
- Write guest posts or articles for blogs, magazines, newspapers, trade journals, or other mediums.

Don't overwhelm yourself by trying to tackle everything at once. Explore the ideas from this list one at a time. You may find that it only takes two or three of these ideas to get your personal brand off of the ground. It'll take some trial and error, and it will most certainly take you outside of your comfort zone. Building a personal brand won't happen overnight. You must be committed for the long haul.

## TAKE ACTION

- ❑ Identify a key soft skill that you need to work on, and create a plan for improving.
- ❑ Set a reminder to create a daily task list that includes three critical tasks related to achieving one of your goals.
- ❑ Take an inventory of the people you currently spend the most time with. Then eliminate toxic relationships and build new relationships.
- ❑ Include exercise in your daily routine.
- ❑ Find a nutritious lifestyle that works for you.
- ❑ Examine your personal goals, and determine if a personal brand will benefit your career.
- ❑ If a personal brand makes sense for your professional career, create an action plan (i.e., build a personal brand website, join online forums, etc.).

# Conclusion

*The biggest adventure you can take is to live the life of your dreams.* —Oprah Winfrey, American media executive and philanthropist

If you're reading this, I want to personally thank you for making it all the way to the end. This is a huge accomplishment, and it means a lot to me that you spent so much of your valuable time with me. I really hope you'll consider my advice from Part 4 of this book and continue to grow personally and professionally.

So what did you think? I want to hear from you. Did this book help you get more out of your internship than you expected? Was there anything you ran into that we didn't cover together in this book? The good, the bad, the ugly—I want to know it all. Send me a personal message, and let me know how your internship and start of your professional career have gone. I take the time to read each and every email I receive. Your feedback and success stories mean so much to me. You can reach me at ryan@ryanglick.com.

I wish you the best of luck with your career and your journey into personal growth. I hope our paths cross again at some point in the near future, and if so, I look forward to hearing about how great your life has been. All the best, and thanks again!

# About the Author

Ryan Glick has been heavily involved in the world of information technology and entrepreneurship since the early 2000s. From small business consulting to Fortune 500 IT leadership, Ryan has a wide array of industry knowledge. He earned his BBA from the University of Iowa in 2004, majoring in management information systems, and his MBA from the University of Iowa in 2009, with a focus on management and marketing. When he's not spending time with his wife and three young children, you'll find Ryan pounding away at his keyboard, doing some sort of crazy exercise program, or listening to a good audiobook or podcast.